TAKE C

OF YOUR LIFE

C000050914

TAKE CONTROL OF YOUR LIFE

How to Control Fate, Luck, Chaos, Karma,
and Life's Other Unruly Forces

Dr. Richard Shoup
with Barry Lenson

McGraw-Hill

New York   San Francisco   Washington, D.C.   Auckland   Bogotá
Caracas   Lisbon   London   Madrid   Mexico City   Milan
Montreal   New Delhi   San Juan   Singapore
Sydney   Tokyo   Toronto

Library of Congress Cataloging-in-Publication Data

Shoup, Richard.
    Take control of your life : how to control fate, luck, chaos, karma, and life's other unruly forces / Richard Shoup; with Barry Lenson.
        p. cm.
    Includes index.
    ISBN 0-07-135207-4 (alk. paper)
    1. Control (Psychology).   2. Choice (Psychology).   I. Lenson, Barry.   II. Title.

BF611.S47   2000
158.1—dc21   99-053278

McGraw-Hill

A Division of The **McGraw·Hill** *Companies*

Copyright © 2000 by Dr. Richard Shoup and Barry Lenson. All rights reserved. Printed in the United States of America. Except as permitted under the United States Copyright Act of 1976, no part of this publication may be reproduced or distributed in any form or by any means, or stored in a database or retrieval system, without the prior written permission of the publisher.

1 2 3 4 5 6 7 8 9 0 AGM/AGM 9 0 9 8 7 6 5 4 3 2 1 0 9

ISBN 0-07-135207-4

It was set in Esprit Book by Inkwell Publishing Services.

Printed and bound by Quebecor/Martinsburg.

McGraw-Hill books are available at special quantity discounts to use as premiums and sales promotions, or for use in corporate training programs. For more information, please write to the Director of Special Sales, McGraw-Hill, 11 West 19th Street, New York, NY 10011. Or contact your local bookstore.

 This book is printed on recycled, acid-free paper containing a minimum of 50 % recycled, de-inked fiber.

To Catherine

CONTENTS

PREFACE

My old choral conducting instructor from high school used to say, "Everything in life is either a frustration or an opportunity!" I had very little idea what he meant then, but I do now. Life is very difficult. It is my sincere hope that this book will give those who read it a better way of relating to the events and fateful happenstance around them.

We may not have much control over the unruly forces of fate, but we can certainly make our lives better and easier by being prepared—and not fighting everything that comes our way. The right kind of outlook, preparation, and actions really can make the difference in whether we are in control of our lives or needlessly victimized.

One day I watched my fellow passengers on a crowded bus. People were standing in the aisles, and many had bulky coats and umbrellas with them. It was a windy and rainy day. One gentleman in particular caught my attention. He was seated, and right in front of him was a rather large person with an umbrella hanging from his arm. Every time the bus moved, the end of the umbrella hit the seated man's leg ever so slightly. I watched in utter amazement as the seated man fumed and glared at the totally unaware umbrella torturer. This went on for some time—longer than I would have thought possible—until the man with the offending bumbershoot left the bus.

I think of this poor, helpless creature from time to time. But was he so helpless after all?

Was there nothing he could have done to end his plight? Could he have summoned his courage, or his most mannerly expression, to ask the man to be a little more careful? Could he have simply moved his leg and avoided the collision? Could he have decided that it was really a good joke and played along?

Anything would have been better than his passive solution, which was not only painful, but also so ineffective. If such a simple situation was a problem, imagine what this person goes through on a given day!

OPPORTUNITY THINKING

In a similar way, we are all buffeted by circumstances. The old bumper sticker "Stuff Happens" is certainly true. In the face of all our daily problems and hurdles to be overcome, many of us are blessed with positive expectations. Others of us are sure only bad things will occur.

Consider this story.

Not long ago I was waiting on line at a convenience store that sold dozens of different lotto cards and games of chance. A woman at the head of the line was picking out many different kinds of gambling instruments. She had placed an enormous wad of bills on the counter to pay for her purchases.

When she turned around, I noticed first of all how sad she looked. Then I noticed a big white cast on her arm. That was not a lucky sign. Later in the parking lot, she got into a very old and rusty car.

I thought that she probably had been playing games of chance for a long time, probably to her detriment. Then I thought maybe her "hope against hope" was keeping her alive and expectant. But as I drove away, I kept thinking how that hope could have been better used.

And that is exactly what I want for the readers of this book.

Each of us has a number of hopes and dreams. We are also stuck with some limits and some patterns that hold us back. Many of these impediments can be changed if we understand ourselves better, and if we can get a realistic understanding of the universe rather than feeling devoid of hope.

In a sense, this book is about opportunities and courage. Its content is largely derived from a lecture series I presented at Marble Collegiate Church in New York City, called "Opportunity Thinking."

Opportunity Thinking is the crux of what this book is about. I was inspired to write it after observing how many of my clients in psychotherapy had such different reactions to happenings in their lives. Some seemed to do so much with so little that I was filled with awe and respect for them. Others seemed to have so much good in their lives, and yet they crabbed and complained at every step of the way. In the end, they did very little with all the good things they had been given.

How could that be, and what could be done to improve the situation?

PREFACE

I hope this book will help many to figure out for themselves how to make the very best of their lives.

YOU CAN TAKE CONTROL OF YOUR LIFE

When I was a boy, my best friend in the neighborhood was Howard, one of the few Jewish people in my small Midwestern town. One day in Sunday school, I picked up the notion that Howard was in trouble.

In class, we were talking about "being saved" (whatever that meant) and the teacher told us one day that people had to be Christians in order for that to happen. I ran with the news to Howard, who was understandably upset. Then I asked my mother whether Howard needed to be saved. To her credit, she didn't know what to say.

Yet as kids often do, Howard and I took care of the problem ourselves. We decided all adults were slightly crazy and it would be best to view the issue of salvation with a proverbial "grain of salt."

I thank Howard, and my own good sense, for that!

Thanks to that experience, somewhere in my heart I realized that no one person or belief system holds the keys to a happy, fulfilling life—not to mention salvation! I realized that "accidents" such as birth, nature, and nurture can never determine the exact and final course of anyone's life—certainly not mine and hopefully not yours.

This has been one of the most valuable lessons I have ever learned. It is only a small part of the unfolding mystery you and I will explore in the pages and chapters that follow.

DR. RICHARD SHOUP

ACKNOWLEDGMENTS

There are so many people to thank in a book like this. I am deeply indebted to the many people I have been privileged to work with over the years, the hundreds of clients in therapy from whom I have learned so much.

I also go back to the many educational experiences I have had, and want to thank the mentors and colleagues who have meant a lot to my evolution and growth. I am particularly indebted to my friends and partners in the Vocare Group, Nina Frost and Ken Ruge, and to other therapists with whom I work at the Counseling Center in Bronxville, New York.

I have also been supported and challenged by the staff and members of several churches in the New York area: the Madison Avenue Presbyterian Church, Marble Collegiate Church, and the Reformed Church of Bronxville. These wonderful churches have taught me the meaning of community and the value of honest and persistent searching after truth and love.

ACKNOWLEDGMENTS

Publishing is a new endeavor for me, and I have needed and received much help from a number of people. My agent, Gareth Esersky of the Carol Mann Agency, understood this book and its promise from the very first. My editor, Betsy Brown at McGraw-Hill, has been encouraging all along the way. Finally, my writer/editor, Barry Lenson, not only writes with ease and grace, but lives his life in the same way. He was always interested, full of good ideas and humor, and he got things done on time!

Finally, I would like to thank my wife, Catherine, the love of my life, who was a booster and a critic at the same time. She keeps my feet on the ground and my head out of the clouds, all the while implying that I am almost wonderful. A difficult balance, to be sure. The luckiest day of my life was the day I met her. And the smartest day of my life was when we decided to get married.

D o you believe that your ability to lead the life you want is impeded by fate, bad luck, bad karma, and other forces that overturn your plans and goals? The first step to get in control is to understand the forces that we sense are standing in our way. We need to know the "enemy" better (perhaps to see that there is no enemy at all), if we are to build the life we desire.

DR. RICHARD SHOUP

1 THRIVE ON CHAOS

The moment Joanne comes through the door, her husband Mark can see she's had a terrible day at work.

"It was total chaos," she says with a sigh. "Nothing but constant interruptions all day long. I never got to any of my top-priority jobs. I never got started on my presentation for next week. It was total anarchy!"

Mark, trying to make things seem a little better, asks whether things might turn out to be any better tomorrow.

"No way," Joanne answers, somewhat angrily. "I can absolutely predict that it will be chaos again tomorrow—you can count on it. It will never change!"

Paradoxically, we can count on chaos today. We all have learned to live with ringing phones, constant interruptions, and an unceasing barrage of new information, ideas, and input. And amid all the hubbub, we feel frustrated, irritated, bewildered, and confused.

We want to get back to the days when life seemed more controllable, predictable, and calm. We want to fill our lives with things we can predict and count on.

Instead, we're losing our sense of control and predictability.

In part, our feelings of frustration and irritability are the result of the ever-expanding range of options available to us today. Not many years ago, you would send your son to the grocery store to buy a box of breakfast cereal. He'd go to the shelf where cereals were displayed and pick up a box of Cheerios or the other brand your family put on the table most mornings.

Today, your child is confronted with a display of breakfast cereal that is a city block long. Which of the 300 choices should your poor kid make? Even the boxes, by virtue of their neon-hued package designs, are hardly distinguishable from each other. There is so much variety that the sensation of variety disappears.

Your poor kid is bombarded by a staggering range of choices.

CHAPTER ONE

SEEKING PATTERNS

Faced with so many choices within complex systems, our first impulse is often to try to establish some kind of order and control. Consider the voice mail systems we all have to use.

Not long ago when my friend Karen's computer went on the fritz, she called the computer maker's customer service line and was greeted with a message that told her, "Press 3 if you have such-and-such a product . . . press 4 if you are using Windows 95 . . .press 5 if you are using Windows 98 . . ." On it went. Finally, like a ball bouncing its way down through a pinball machine, Karen landed in some slot and got to speak with a human being who put Karen on hold, suggested she try this and that—and ultimately did not solve the problem.

So Karen had to call back several times. Yet by the third call, she had devised a strategy to control that chaotic voice mail system. She learned that by pressing 3, 5, 7, and 8, she could quickly worm her way through the system and connect to a customer service rep.

In her small way, Karen was trying to establish a pattern that would lend order to a system that, from her outsider's vantage point, was unordered and chaotic.

More than ever before, we try to discern patterns in chaos. Yet the fact is, the search for order is anything but new. In his writings and his televised specials on the power of myth, Joseph Campbell elegantly shows how myth—including parables of death, resurrection, magical plants and places, journeys to the underworld, and other miraculous events—really represents an attempt to comprehend life's seemingly unordered events.

Death, birth, evil, and good—all these can be made more intelligible through parable and the force of imagination.

The Head of the Cat

In his famous introduction to the Princeton University Press edition of the *I Ching,* or *Chinese Book of Change,* Carl Jung makes a telling observation about human perception. He writes about a man who is sitting in a room. The door to the room is open only a crack. Outside the room, a cat is walking back and forth and the man can see the cat's pacing only though the door's slitlike opening.

Looking at the cat that way, the man thinks, "The cat's head is causing its tail."

Of course, a cat's head does *not* cause its tail, no matter where it is walking.

The slit in the door is like the time window through which we all view life's larger events. Something happens today, and we believe it causes what happens tomorrow. That's the slit we're looking through—one that makes us understand large events in terms of cause and effect.

The fact is, some events are not made up of different causal segments. Some, like the walking cat, are part of larger processes which lie beyond the range of our perceptions. Sometimes, we need to let the whole cat pass before we know it is a cat at all—before we can fully apprehend the forces at work in our lives. Our perception is too limited to see the bigger picture.

In a sense, that's what religion is all about—trying to make sense of world systems that appear aimless, violent, full of random events. On one level, Genesis—the starting scriptural point of all Judeo-Christian religions—represents an attempt to come to terms with the presence of evil in the world.

In the Christian faith in Jesus, the Jewish expectancy of a coming messiah, the Islamic belief in Mohammed, and the Buddhist belief in the great sage, the world's major faiths seek insight from powerful figures who are uniquely empowered to teach lesser mortals that the world is not out of control, but comprehensible. Even the disorderly forces of evil and sin can be banished and our lives can be made whole.

ORDER AND SCIENCE

The history of science can also be seen as an ongoing attempt to bring incomprehensible, disorderly events into the realm of the understandable and regularized.

The pursuit was recorded in ancient times.

Pythagoras of Samos (c. 560–480 B.C.), discovered that vibrating strings produce harmonious tones when their lengths can be compared in the most basic numerical relationships, such as 2:1, 3:2, and 4:3. Pythagorians also believed that the planets vibrated according to the same ratios—the "music of the spheres" that was further explored by Kepler 2000 years later.

Aristotle (384–322 B.C.), created a science of logic to lend order to the disarrayed process of human thought itself. In the natural sciences, he attempted to codify the complex relationship between matter and the processes of change that transform it.

Lucretius (c. 95–55 B.C.), the Roman philosopher, strove to free people's minds from superstition by explaining the elements of matter in scientific terms.

Then, in the sixteenth and seventeenth centuries, there was a virtual explosion of new scientific exploration and discovery.

The Statue's Eyes

I recently hailed a cab driver in New York City who told me a fascinating story. A native of Cairo, Egypt, he described a honeymoon trip he and his wife had taken to the Valley of the Kings.

"Once a year," he told me, "the first rays of the rising sun fall upon the eyes of the statue of one of the pharaohs who are buried in a massive tomb."

The driver and his wife visited the tomb on that date. Before dawn, they and other tourists walked down a long, dark hallway and stood in the darkness by the statue. Sure enough, the moment the sun rose, a beam of sunlight shot down the dark hallway and fell precisely on the eyes of the pharaoh.

"It was a moment that changed my life," my cab driver told me.

The ancients were well able to amass huge amounts of complex information and lend order to it. Their feats still astound us today.

Francis Bacon (1561–1626), in a treatise called Instauratio Magna, set out on a daunting course: to empower humankind to gain mastery of nature. Though considered more of a philosopher than a scientist, Bacon pushed forward the boundaries of human knowledge of the chaotic and uncertain.

Galileo Galilei (1564–1642) dropped various objects from the Leaning Tower of Pisa and showed that Aristotle was wrong when he assumed that the speed of an object's fall was proportional to its weight. In 1604, when a supernova appeared in the sky, Galileo engaged in heated battle with other philosophers who held that change in the heavens was impossible. He reshaped the landscape of human thought.

Johannes Kepler (1571–1634) reclaimed the Pythagorean concept of the "music of the spheres" and, using modern telescopes, attempted to define harmonic ratios in the distances between the planets and the sun.

René Descartes (1596–1649) postulated that humans are made of mind and body—two distinct materials. He might well be called the father of psychology—the ongoing attempt to understand the bewildering universe within each of us.

Sir Isaac Newton (1643–1727), a towering figure of modern science, explored a staggering variety of scientific questions, including optics, calculus, gravity, and astronomy. When he saw that famous apple falling to the ground, he embarked on a path of inquiry that led him to conclude that the earth's gravity extended as far as the moon, holding it in orbit. Incomprehensible forces and events, through his keen mind, were brought into the boundaries of accepted human knowledge.

What an explosion of human inquiry runs through this galloping little history of scientific thought! Faced with complex and seemingly random events, all those great scientists were seeking to find order. They were looking for laws and patterns that could be repeated.

If evidence can be repeated, a pattern can emerge. Ideas and laws can be proved. And the veil of darkness between the knowable and the unknowable can be pushed back a few paces more with each experiment that gathers new data.

Yet all these thinkers—and more recent scientists too— were also forced to confront a troubling reality. In the search for order, progress was being made. At the same time, certain things just didn't fit.

- Two identical balls dropped from the same place in just the same way didn't necessarily land in exactly the same place or at the same speed.

- Identical amounts of two reacting elements, combined in just the same way, produced surprisingly different amounts of heat.

- A ping-pong ball, bobbing in a stream of steady air, did not eventually start to make a predictable range of repetitive motions. Its motions were erratic, unpatterned, unrepeated, and chaotic.

So what did scientists do when confronted with outcomes like that—results that seemed to fall outside the realm of predictability or quantitative analysis? They chose to ignore the problem. The shadow side of science, in fact, embodies a story of realities that have been conveniently left out of the boundaries of well-defined experiments.

This was the case, at least, until the start of our own century, when science enlarged its scope enough to admit the existence of the undefinable and the uncertain.

THE BIRTH OF CHAOS THEORY

The process of "factoring in" unpredictable elements began scarcely four decades ago, with one of the greatest discoveries in the history of science—chaos theory. In its own way, chaos theory is just as important a field of inquiry as relativity or quantum physics.

In his remarkable, and very readable book *Chaos: Making a New Science* (Penguin Books, 1987), James Gleick reports that the birth of chaos theory took place, more or less, at the Los Alamos National Laboratory and MIT in the 1960s and 1970s. Scientists, including Mitchell Feigenbaum and

Edward Lorenz, were not only beginning to admit that irregularities were to be expected in science, but with the help of new machines called computers, they were grappling with the problem of studying those irregularities.

They were starting to look for order, if you will, in events that were by their nature disorderly. As Gleick writes about Lorenz's experiments at MIT in the 1960s:

> The simulated weather in Edward Lorenz's new electronic computer changed slowly but certainly, drifting through a permanent dry midday midseason, as if the world had turned into Camelot, or some particularly bland version of southern California.
>
> Outside his window Lorenz could watch real weather, the early-morning fog creeping along the Massachusetts Institute of Technology campus or the low clouds slipping over the rooftops from the Atlantic. Fog and clouds never arose in the model running on his computer. The machine, a Royal McBee, was a thicket of wiring and vacuum tubes that occupied an ungainly portion of Lorenz's office, made a surprising and irritating noise, and broke down every week or so. It had neither the speed nor the memory to manage a realistic simulation of the earth's atmosphere and oceans. Yet Lorenz created a toy weather in 1960 that succeeded in mesmerizing his colleagues. Every minute the machine marked the passing of a day by printing a row of numbers across a page. If you knew how to read the printouts, you would see a prevailing westerly wind swing now to the north, now to the south, now back to the north. Digitized cyclones spun slowly around an idealized globe. As word spread through the department, the other meteorologists would gather around with the

graduate students, making bets on what Lorenz's weather would do next. Somehow, nothing ever happened the same way twice.

It is hardly any wonder that Lorenz, high-minded scientist that he was, chose to simulate something so widespread and mundane as a weather system. Weather was, and still remains, one of the most complicated and chaotic systems. Weather was a prime candidate for study as a chaotic system.

In those days, meteorologists were not able to predict weather very accurately. On television, the weatherperson was often a kind of stand-up comedian who poked fun at his or her own profession. Meteorologists knew the barest outlines of how to predict weather. They knew that winter is colder than summer. And they knew that weather systems—cold, rain, snow—usually traveled from west to east across the country. So if it was raining in Ohio on a Monday, the weatherperson on the evening news in New York would step before the cameras and predict rain for Tuesday.

Along comes Edward Lorenz, with his discovery that even in a steady-state computerized system, odd variations took place. Even in electronic simulation, uncertain winds could blow. Then, one day, something so remarkable occurred that it might arguably be called the moment when chaos theory was born. As Gleick writes:

> One day in the winter of 1961, wanting to examine one sequence at greater length, Lorenz took a shortcut. Instead of starting the whole run over, he started midway through. To give the machine its initial conditions, he typed the numbers straight from the earlier printout. Then he walked down the hall to get away from the noise and drink a cup of coffee. When he returned an

hour later, he saw something unexpected, something that planted a seed for a new science.

This new run should have exactly duplicated the old. Lorenz had copied the numbers into the machine himself. The program had not changed. Yet as he stared at the new printout, Lorenz saw his weather diverging so rapidly from the pattern of the last run that, within just a few months, all resemblance had disappeared. He looked at one set of numbers, then back at the other. He might as well have chosen two random weathers out of a hat. His first thought was that another vacuum tube had gone bad.

Suddenly he realized the truth. There had been no malfunction. The problem lay in the numbers he had typed. In the computer's memory, six decimal places were stored: .506127. On the printout, to save space, just three appeared: .506. Lorenz had entered the shorter, rounded-off numbers, assuming that the difference— one part in a thousand—was inconsequential.

It was a reasonable assumption. If a weather satellite can read ocean-surface temperature to within one part in a thousand, its operators consider themselves lucky. Lorenz's Royal McBee was implementing the classical program. It used a purely deterministic system of equations. Given a particular starting point, the weather would unfold exactly the same way each time. Given a slightly different starting point, the weather should unfold in a slightly different way. A small numerical error was like a small puff of wind—surely the small puffs faded or canceled each other out before they could change important, large-scale features of the weather. Yet in Lorenz's particular system of equations, small errors proved catastrophic.

He decided to look more closely at the way two nearly identical runs of weather flowed apart. He copied one of the wavy lines of output onto a transparency and laid it over the other, to inspect the way it diverged. First, two humps matched detail for detail. Then one line began to lag a hairsbreadth behind. By the time the two runs reached the next hump, they were distinctly out of phase. By the third or fourth hump, all similarity had vanished.

It was only a wobble from a clumsy computer. Lorenz could have assumed something was wrong with his particular machine or his particular model—probably *should* have assumed. It was not as though he had mixed sodium and chlorine and got gold.

But for reasons of mathematical intuition that his colleagues would begin to understand only later, Lorenz felt a jolt: something was philosophically out of joint. The practical import could be staggering.

Now, Lorenz had a computer that was as big as a room. (Probably it was about as powerful as the one that sits on your desk today—possibly less so.) He put some numbers into it and went down the hall for a cup of coffee. And when he returned, his life had shot off into totally new areas.

By omitting an inconsequential string of numbers, he had triggered chaos.

The Butterfly Effect

This experience led to the identification of something called the "butterfly effect." It holds that if a butterfly in China flaps its wings, it changes the weather pattern over Europe. The change may not be great, or even a change that can be measured. But the change is as real as a tornado coursing down the main street of a Kansas town.

CHAPTER ONE

The underlying message? Small, fateful events, taken over time, set off shock waves that have the potential to change our lives.

The Minister's Story

Not long ago, I was speaking with a minister of a church in the New York area, and he told me a remarkable story. About 40 years ago, someone had the foresight to give to the church a donation of about $50,000, which was a lot of money back then.

So the church set up an endowment fund and the money accrued interest over the years. As people became aware of the fund's existence, they were motivated to contribute too. The minister told me, "Today, we have $12 million in that fund. We stay within our operating budget, and we give away the income from that $12 million to people in our community who really need it. So our church has an incredible effect because of that one person's generous act, which made it all possible."

Now, there's the butterfly effect in operation. Any action we take sets up a ripple in the universe and causes other things to happen. We never act alone. When we take any step—no matter how small—fate moves with us.

Why Worry About Chaos?

At this point in the chapter, you may be wondering, "This is all very interesting, but why should I give a darn about chaos? What's the benefit in worrying about something that I can't effectively understand or control?"

In response to these questions, let me offer two suggestions. First, you can do a lot to control chaos, as we'll see in the next few pages. Chaos may not be quite as unruly as we expect. Second, you can experience a liberating sense of control in your life when you realize that chaos—though unset-

Another Butterfly, Another Effect

A Sound of Thunder, a short story written by Ray Bradbury in 1952, tells about a butterfly effect of a different sort. In this story, which projects time travel as a reality in the twenty-first century, a big-game hunter named Eckels takes a trip six million years back in time to hunt dinosaurs. The dinosaur tour company has set up special walkways and protected areas for dinosaur-hunting, and the only dinosaurs that can be killed are those that are about to die anyway.

All tourists are given a strong warning: They are absolutely forbidden to leave protected areas or touch any living thing. But at the sight of a charging Tyrannosaurus Rex, Eckels panics and runs into the jungle. After a while, he comes back to the time-travel machine and returns to the twenty-first century.

When Eckels gets home, he's in for a shock. Everything is strangely changed. Even the English language has been altered almost beyond recognition.

"Why did this happen?" Eckels wonders. Then he looks down at his boots, caked with mud. He finds a tiny butterfly there, squashed during his panicky run through the jungle.

The death of that butterfly has altered the shape of the future. Why? Perhaps because the lizard that would have eaten it died from hunger before he got to reproduce, which led to other repercussions on and on through time. Over time, the effect of that one tiny death was cataclysmic. It's science fiction, of course, but also scientific reality. Any small action we take changes all time to come.

tling—is not about to ruin your life or wrest control from your hands.

With the right outlook, we can make a friend of chaos, end its ability to unsettle us and even reap its rewards.

A New Way to Look at Chaos

I've already devoted a good deal of attention in this chapter to the history of science, including the birth of chaos theory. In light of those considerations, I'd like to share what I consider to be a rather liberating reality: *There is no chaos. There is a pattern in everything. We just need the right lens to see it.*

The history of science shows that the boundaries of human knowledge and science are always being pushed back. Forces that were perceived as chaotic in years past are always migrating into the realm of the quantifiable, predictable, understood, and routine. This is the basic mechanism of science.

- Weather, long thought to be chaotic and unpredictable, can now be predicted with remarkable precision.

- Human longevity, once believed to be determined by God alone, is increasingly determined by the efforts of medicine.

On the list could go.

Will chaos disappear entirely? Absolutely not. Yet the farther it is driven to the margins of human knowledge, the heartier it will become. There will always be more unruly knowledge to be integrated into our understanding.

After all, chaos is always waiting there in the wings.

- On a calm day, a tornado suddenly blows up—the result of many small forces that individually were too

---

One Reason Life Is Not Boring

If totally predictable, life would be terribly boring.

Even chaos has patterns—very beautiful patterns, like those swirling Raster graphics that are randomly generated by computers.

You can weave yourself into those patterns. Every step you take toward fate makes a difference in your life.

---

small for scientific instruments to perceive. It was unpredictable, yet it happened.

- While gambling at a casino, a woman improbably wins a series of long-shot bets. There's no understanding why—it's simply the hand that chaos is dealing her. A sudden confluence of odds and events.

- A man who has been diagnosed with a terminal disease miraculously recovers. Some minute, chaotic forces are at work—forces that have not yet been perceived or understood by researchers. The scope of their lens needs to be widened.

- Walking down the street, you run into a friend you haven't seen in 15 years. She could just have easily walked down the next block and you would have missed her. Yet some odd confluence puts her there in your path—and your meeting is a welcome gift from chaos.

Viewed from such perspectives, chaos enriches our lives. It's a puzzling, frustrating, wonder-filled companion that, plunking for us from the sidelines, adds meaning and wonder to life.

Chaos Can Lead to Health

In my practice as a psychotherapist, I am always on the alert when someone tells me, "I feel totally lost. I have no idea where I am supposed to go. I don't know what my life is supposed to be."

Often, people who express these sentiments have recently encountered something unsettling in their lives—the loss of a job, a separation from a spouse. At such times, I can barely restrain myself from saying, "Good! In an open space, you can move."

Chaos can free us from the constraints of predictable routines. It can usher in a period of intense personal growth. The transition points, when things are chaotic and open, are the times when things can really change in our lives.

HOW TO THRIVE ON CHAOS

We need to learn to thrive on chaos. We shouldn't be running away from it. With the right outlook, we can actually prosper in it. Let's take a look at how.

Expect chaos. The first step toward thriving on chaos is to learn to expect it. Attitudes like these can help:

- *Remind yourself each day that your plans are likely to be interrupted or changed.* Expect and welcome disorder. You can't predict everything—a fact that will no longer unsettle you if can adopt a chaos-friendly mindset.

- *Wield your will in an egoless way.* Learn to say, "Here's what I'd like to see happen, but I'm open to unex-

pected messages and events too." If you think everything is going to go your way all the time, you will be
fighting life constantly.

- *Don't worry about mistakes.* To move ahead in life, you
  need to fail and make mistakes. As Carl Jung said,
  "The way to wholeness is through fitful starts and
  wrong turnings." If you don't have the courage to try
  things that might fail, you're not growing or living fully.

No doubt about it. The people who accomplish the most
are also those who risk the most in the face of chaotic outcomes. To live our lives more fully, we may even have to cultivate our ability to courageously make mistakes.

We can be like a prizefighter who doesn't know what his
opponent is about to do. But he is constantly ready to adapt
to changes, ready for something new. By learning to contin-
uously expect the unexpected, we can exhibit grace under
pressure and even welcome challenging or unexpected
events.

Enjoy chaos and stop catastrophizing. Try to remember that unexpected change is not necessarily a setback. Even
seemingly negative events—like the loss of a job or an unexpected illness—are rarely so devastating that our whole
world will end. Unwelcome events often turn into something
wonderful.

Chaos can bring needed messages that good change is
about to occur. Our lives are about to move onto a path that
is more authentic and rewarding.

**Set aside opinions and cherished beliefs, and
embrace ambiguity**. Certainty is a kind of mental rigor
mortis that makes us unable to adapt to change in our lives.
Instead, we can question ourselves at every turn by asking,

> **Thriving on Chaos**
>
> In his book *Thriving on Chaos* (HarperCollins, 1989), Tom Peters observes that corporations today are changing so fast that there is no time to understand everything. By the time change is understood, it's often too late to do anything about what has changed. Knowledge becomes obsolete faster today than at any time in history.
>
> The only way to keep up with such rapid change is to move as rapidly as the change itself in your thinking, in your ability to adapt.

"Why do I hold this belief?" or "Am I seeing the bigger picture here, or missing it because of the lens I'm using to frame this problem?"

Develop a "big world" mind. The more chaos you can welcome into your thinking—paradoxically—the wiser your conclusions about the world can become. Buddhists call this the "big world" mind. It's the mind that sees the wider picture, as well as our place in it.

When we do not place ourselves at the center of our universe, we take an important step forward. Since we see ourselves in the context of larger events and forces, we become free to be more playful with a world where we are just one participant in a larger, more interesting interplay.

Meet life in a nonlinear fashion. By welcoming disruptions and sudden changes of direction in our activities, we align ourselves with larger processes of change. We begin thinking along discontinuous lines. When we do, we are more receptive to unconscious messages, to fate, to insights and hunches. We might even become more receptive to God's or a higher power's will in our lives.

Not every change of direction is a setback—even when such a shift causes us to rethink a project we are working on, start a new career, or make other abrupt changes of course in our lives and work. Sometimes, they are part of a larger and more important process of interplay with the world.

Be alert for opportunities that chaos brings. Every day is full of seemingly random events. The phone rings on the job, and we speak with a colleague or contact from outside our company. We attend a meeting and talk to people we know as well as to others we are getting to know for the first time. We go to a convention and enjoy in-depth conversations with people we have never met before. Opportunities often arise from these random occurrences—and that's a fascinating reality if we stop to think about it. With the right outlook, we can turn chaotic events into opportunities.

Be sensitive to situations that hold special opportunity. If you are on the alert, opportunities stand out. If you walk into a routine meeting and the company president is unexpectedly sitting there, for example, you might have been given an opportunity to shine.

Remember that "mundane" events may offer hidden opportunities. The fact is, opportunity-bearing events often seem routine, and you have to be on the alert for them. Taking consistent actions to do your best in many seemingly routine situations is like casting the proverbial "loaves upon the waters." It's the butterfly effect at work again. You never know when, or how, but your good acts will be returned to you in beneficial ways.

The Richest Woman in New York

It was a spring evening in New York City, and I was walking down the street, on my way to move my car because of parking regulations. I passed a woman on a park bench. I kept walking. Half an hour later I had to move my car again and I saw this woman a second time.

She looked me in the eye and smiled. She was about 80 years old.

I said, "Nice evening."

She smiled and said, "Yes, it's a beautiful evening. I love to come out here this time of year because I can begin to sense that spring is coming. The trees. The blossoms. I can smell the earth. I just know that spring is coming. I just love it."

I said, "Thank you very much. You have really made my night."

All my irritation about my car and all that stuff vanished because of this ten-second encounter. Our plans won't always carry us to where we need to go. We need to step back and let in something unexpected. We need to be open to the unexpected. That night, I met one of the richest women on the Upper East Side.

Take heart and have courage. In reading the points I make above, you might have surmised that learning to thrive on chaos should be a rather lighthearted, joyous process.

It is, but it has a tougher side too. Thriving on chaos is not like taking a walk in the park. It often takes a lot of alienation, depression, loneliness—even despair. Sometimes we have to pull away from people, question our own beliefs in disquieting ways, and take a new look at relationships.

Sometimes, we have to leave a job we have been happy at for many years, or we simply cannot grow.

Enter into the spirit of your vision. Here's a step that can help generate the courage needed to walk this unsettling path. Through chaos and change, you will create something better with your life.

If you are pursuing a specific goal or agenda, you can dwell on the feelings of elation that the vision of it brings to you. You're entering into uncertainty so that you can become a painter, or start a company, or get married. Such bright images can act like beacons to guide you forward through unhappy times and the turbulent forces of chaos.

Even if you do not know just where you would like your life to lead, your vision can lead you forward. Perhaps you want to envision the better place that lies ahead in general ways—as your heart's desire, as a shining high plateau, or through whatever imagery appeals to you. Whether highly specific or inexplicit, your vision will allow you to feel centered and aware that chaos and change are not forces that will pull you from your real life path.

Chaos is not an enemy. Its unexpected forces provide the change and forward momentum that allow us to live our lives most completely.

EXERCISES

1. **Try to live one day with a playful outlook.** If possible, focus this exercise on a typical day at work. Instead of obsessing or worrying about every inter-

ruption or unexpected event, treat it as a happy and unexpected message.

Of course, you cannot treat every workday in just this way, but trying it for a day or two can produce a stimulating and interesting change in the way you perceive the pacing and order of a typical day. You may even find, as I did the first time I tried this experiment, that you become better attuned to the real messages that chaos is bringing you. You thought your priority for the day was to write a long report, for example, but then you are interrupted ten times so you can handle problems with several customers.

Perhaps chaos is telling you that your perceived priority is not the correct one—the one the "fates had in store" for that day. A playful, open outlook often deepens your perception of such underlying trends.

2. **"Throw a pebble" and see what ripples come back to you.** Single out one action you can take in response to chaos. Take it, and stay attuned to what results from it.

If you're attending a large party where you know only a few people, for example, single out one or two guests and decide to really connect with them. Introduce yourself, share a few stories about who you are and what you do, and see what evolves. Most often, you will find that something interesting will evolve from such chance encounters, yielded up to you by chaos. You and your new friends might have acquaintances in common. You might be able to offer each other needed advice about career, family, or other matters. Lasting friendships might even evolve.

By taking small actions in chaos, you will see that chaos may not be as random or disorderly as you believe. Within arbitrary events and situations, you will begin to see patterns.

3. **Don't make a decision about something.** For take-charge people, especially, this can be a real test!

   Let's say your teenager has been accepted by three or four colleges and you're tempted to say, "Go to Columbia! It's a great school." Or let's say you and your spouse have been shopping for a new home. You've narrowed your search down to two houses, and you're at the point of saying, "I think that colonial is the better choice. Let's make an offer on it."

   Instead of taking those actions, try to stand back for a time and watch the processes unfold. Your teenager will make a decision about which college to attend, and tell you. Your spouse will tell you which house he or she feels is the best choice—or the decision may be made for you by a leaky roof, a seller who takes the house off the market, or other unexpected events.

   By failing to act—not in all things, of course, but as an experiment—you are better able to observe processes at work that lie outside of your own will and control. Often, the outcomes of seemingly chaotic processes will astonish you.

4. **Create a list of chaotic events that have intruded on your life.** Look back a long way as you write this list—10, 20, 30 years or more.

   Create a list of unexpected, surprising things that chaos brought to you. Then add the outcomes of those events. Your list might include events like these:

— I met a man who offered me a job. *Result:* That job became my career.

— I lost my job. *Result:* I entered the teaching profession.

— I fell and broke my leg. *Result:* Thanks to the program of physical therapy that was required, I began an exercise program and got in much better shape.

— I entered a raffle at my church and won a personal computer back in 1985. *Result:* I was the first person in my work group to start using a PC and I am still ahead of the pack as far as computer skills are concerned.

Through this exercise, you will find that seemingly random, chaotic events are usually part of some larger process—a process that you can only understand later on. Armed with this insight, you may find you are better able to cope with the "knocks and bumps" life deals you today. Each one may be a gift in disguise, waiting to reveal its true nature.

2 BECOME A MASTER OF LUCK

On August 9, 1945, an American B-29 bomber took off from a remote island in the Pacific Ocean. An atomic bomb was on board and the target was the city of Kokura in Japan. When the plane reached Kokura, the crew found out that the city was socked in by fog. There was no way for them to locate the target. So they went on to follow their backup plan, which was to bomb Nagasaki. As the result of that fog, Nagasaki was bombed and Kokura was spared. The lives of hundreds of thousands of unfortunate people were completely altered by the presence of clouds.

This incident, more than most others I can think of, demonstrates the awesome power that simple luck can play in determining the good and bad things that happen to all of us.

We can have extraordinary luck. We can have terrible luck. We can have runs of good luck, followed by runs of bad luck in our lives. Where does it come from? What does it mean? Is there anything we can do about it?

We took a close look at chaos in the last chapter. Now it is time to turn our attention to luck. How is luck different?

On the surface, luck and chaos might seem to be similar. Both are powerful forces that appear to subject us to a confusing barrage of unconnected events. Both can bring us good things or bad. Perhaps most important, we seem to have control over neither of them.

The difference between chaos and luck is one of interpretation and value setting.

Chaos subjects us to a steady stream of events. We get in our cars in the morning to drive to work. The traffic is heavy (bad luck!) but suddenly eases up just as we approach our exit (good luck!). Or we enter a store and find that the item of clothing we're looking for is out of stock (bad luck!) but then the clerk calls another store and offers to have it delivered to us the next day (bad luck has turned to good!).

More than we might suspect, these valuations are quite subjective. The same events can be interpreted as lucky or unlucky, depending on our needs, impressions, and moods.

Often, when someone who has just lost a job seeks my counsel, his or her first statement is, "What bad luck! What a lousy break!" Then, over time, that interpretation almost always shifts to the opposite view. The same man or woman will inevitably say, "Losing my job was the luckiest thing that could have happened to me."

So we see that the quality of luck resides not in the event itself, but in the way we judge and assign value to it. For the most part—except for outright catastrophes or wonderful godsends—events are neutral. Luck does not exist per se. It is a trick of the human mind.

Where Luck Is Found

Luck resides not so much in the events that surround us per se, as in the interpretations we place on them. It's part of human nature to characterize happenings as good or bad.

Often, the event that seemed negative today turns out to be quite positive tomorrow.

THE EBB AND FLOW OF LUCK

Most of us feel that we've experienced "lucky" and "unlucky" days, not to mention lucky and unlucky "streaks" in our lives. If we get too lucky for a period of time, we expect things to turn around and to enter a period of bad luck.

Good luck, it seems, scares us even more than bad.

When my friend Bill got a clean bill of health after an exhaustive physical examination and tests, he appeared almost worried at the outcome. "It troubles me that they didn't find anything wrong," he told me as he knocked his knuckles against the wooden table while we were having lunch. "Now I'm in for it! Things can only get worse!"

In medieval times, we know, the belief that luck was cyclical was represented by a fictitious machine known as the Wheel of Fortune. When people were fortunate, they felt they were high up on this wheel as it turned. Any period of good luck would inevitably be followed by a period of bad fortune as the wheel cycled them down to its lowest point.

If things got really bad, people took solace from the knowledge that things were about to get better. Their risky lives were ruled by cycles and forces that were beyond their senses and certainly beyond their control.

This kind of outlook about luck seems to be an integral part of human nature. Most of us believe that good luck or bad operates in patterns or cycles. We experience weeks or months when things seem to be going our way—and other times when nothing good seems to be happening. There are periods when we feel supported and lifted up in our work and relationships—and other periods when we feel like we're struggling every step of the way. Some of us even believe we pass through periods when forces of good and evil are exerting their power over us.

Such feelings are part of the allure of luck. When we pass our life experience through this continual judgmental filter—known as luck—we are trying to keep a bead on our elusive relationship with forces well beyond our ken and control.

And many of us test that relationship frequently. Even every day.

When someone spends a dollar for a lottery ticket, what process is really taking place? On the surface, the ticket buyer is making a long-shot wager that could result in substantial winnings. On a deeper level, he's taking a read on where he stands in the universe—trying to establish his status as a fortunate person or an unfortunate one.

Most people, I believe, deeply desire good fortune. They want good things to happen to them. They want it not only because of the specific outcomes that might result—a win of many dollars, a long life, a partnership with a loving spouse—but also because the sense of being fortunate lends a blessed aspect to life.

Most of Us Deeply Desire Good Fortune

We want good things to happen to us. We deeply want our lives to be successful and to mean something. We want the people around us to experience a similar life. Deep down, we're expectant beings.

Are You Lucky or Unlucky?

Are you a lucky or unlucky person? Few people, I think, would dismiss that question as unworthy of consideration. It gives most people pause. Typically, they think for a while and then place themselves somewhere in the middle.

"I don't know. I guess my luck is about average most of the time," says my friend Pauline.

If pressed, a few people will admit that they see themselves as unlucky. And some people own up that they see themselves as lucky and fortunate. That's a wonderful way to feel. All these people usually admit that they have had times of hard luck, and times of good. So there are many different patterns that can emerge from this deceptively simple question—answers that seem revealing and worthy of consideration.

One client who came in to see me years ago told me right off that he had been unlucky in love for more than 20 years.

He actually said it that way. He was a man in his forties—a good-looking, intelligent, winning kind of man. He had enjoyed a good job and an interesting life. Yet for some reason, he was never able to connect with a woman the way he wanted to. He told me in detail about his problems in love relationships. The way he described each situation, with each woman, was shaped and calculated to show me why he was unlucky.

The underlying theme of each relationship he described was that the relationship had gone bad, through no fault of his own. He described himself as an unwitting victim of bad luck and adverse fate. One woman became attracted to a friend of his and "betrayed" him. A second was of another faith, and the differences could not be reconciled. Another had children from a previous marriage—and that represented too much "baggage" for him to cope with.

Using luck, he was trying to explain that he was not at fault for the fact that he was alone.

He was a bright man and I think he realized that he couldn't keep his script going on forever. One of the reasons he came to see me must have been that he was ready to put aside his practice of seeing himself as a passive agent in his life. He was ready to take control.

He was also, at the time, involved in a relationship with someone he really cared for. He wanted help to make it work—to make sure he was not once again the victim of adverse luck. So we worked for months, talking about the relationship. It was not easy or comfortable for him to accept that he had played a part in his long string of failed relationships. Yet with work, he came to see that he had everything to do with what had happened to him over the years. He developed a will to change and began to replace a passive stance with an active one. He took the lead and made his current relationship work.

Once you have a conception of yourself as lucky or unlucky, it's very hard to change that.

Many of us are attached to our self-view as lucky or unlucky. Our ability to shed a negative self-image in regard to luck can be a valuable invitation to take control of our lives and move forward.

The Purpose of Gambling

Gambling is a vehicle many people choose to test the turbulent waters of luck. In fact, we live in a culture that seems exceptionally preoccupied with gambling.

- About 100 million Americans visit gambling casinos every year.

- Lotteries are adding huge sums of money to the coffers of many state governments. Despite the minuscule odds of winning, people line up to give away money they would resist paying in taxes. Then each evening, they turn on their televisions to see if they have won.

- Several tribes of Native Americans who had difficulty establishing an economic base through other businesses have become astonishingly affluent by opening gambling casinos.

- The Friday night poker game—really a gambling ritual—remains an ingrained part of American culture.

- Many retirees spend their later years playing bingo in nursing homes.

- Trading on the stock market has gone from an activity practiced by the "upper crust" of society to something widely practiced among all socioeconomic groups in the United States.

Just Plane Luck

A friend of mine was aboard a commercial airliner several months ago. Sitting next to him were two well-dressed businessmen who did not know each other prior to the flight.

As my friend listened, the two men struck up a conversation about gambling. Each of them visited gambling casinos at least once a month. They exchanged stories about their exploits in playing blackjack and roulette. Suddenly, one of the men said to the other, "Do you think there's an odd number of people on this plane, or an even?"

Within a few minutes, they agreed to bet on it and each man anted up $300.

Then, while my astonished friend watched, the two men counted up the passengers and crew members. Finally they had agreed on a figure for everyone except the people in the cockpit. They asked a flight attendant how many people were up there—and that number determined that the "odd" man won.

My friend observed, "They were pale, sweating, and in a frenzy that seemed nearly erotic. The emotions were running a lot higher than a $300 bet would have led me to expect—even though $300 is hardly peanuts."

In short, the cult of luck has taken on the dimensions of a national religion in America. And the same can be said of most other countries too. A preoccupation with luck seems part of human nature.

On the surface, we might assume that people are obsessed with gambling because it offers a chance to earn vast amounts of money quickly. At the same time, even the most seasoned gamblers know that the chances of consistently scoring really big wins are quite slim. Successful gambling requires hard work.

Successful professional gamblers, in fact, see gambling as a quite practical profession. A good blackjack player knows how to count cards and how to bet. She has reduced the odds of losing to the point where playing the game becomes nearly a practical way for her to earn money.

Getting Lucky

Jack, a fellow I knew in college, would routinely walk up to any young woman he found attractive and ask her out on a date. Most of us were shy about women and held back around them. Not Jack.

"Sooner or later, someone will say yes," he explained to us. "Sooner or later, I'll get lucky." And even though he gained a reputation as a very odd fellow, from time to time he did get a date.

Jack was testing out the waters of life. Was he attractive? Unattractive? Destined to have a relationship in his life, or to live alone? In his own way, he was trying to determine an important aspect of his life. He was testing how the world would treat him in an important life area.

Not surprisingly, people who are addicted to gambling are those who are at the greatest risk of losing—the people who sit mindlessly pumping quarters into slot machines or who buy handfuls of lottery tickets each week with nearly no chances of winning. It follows that there is something more to gambling than a simple desire to win money or a money-earning system that can be learned. Haven't we all heard tales of people who lost family fortunes at the casino—almost as if they were trying to destroy themselves financially?

Compulsive or near-compulsive gambling is not about money. It is a seeking of some message from fate. In a contrary way, it is about self-empowerment. It is often a desperate attempt to turn a life around by seeking for some divine intervention or help.

The Gambler as Tragic Figure

The popular image of compulsive gamblers as tragic, failed beings is not without basis. Many gamblers have pinned their hopes, not on themselves, but on some divine intervention that never arrives.

It is a tragic way to lose control of a life.

Lady Luck

Luck is often portrayed as a seductive, appealing female presence. Equally interesting, casinos have all the outer—and interior—trappings of gaudy brothels.

Perhaps this is because gambling is inherently erotic—or at least, the state it invokes seems erotic. Or perhaps it harks back to some medieval image of a goddess, both erotic and chaste, who imparts good fortune or bad.

Taking Risks: Another Kind of Luck Testing

There is another form of luck testing that is quite prevalent in our culture. It is risk taking.

Many members of our society bungee jump, snowboard, climb rocks, and engage in other hazardous activities—just for the fun of it. Such activities are closely akin to gambling. They are really attempts to experience the odd exhilaration that comes from testing luck and surviving.

Just the other evening as I was driving home, I noticed one of those maniacal tailgaters who seem to travel our roads with increasing frequency. The driver zoomed up only inches behind the bumper of the car ahead of him, then abruptly swerved into another lane and cut off other cars with only inches to spare. Finally, he rocketed off into the distance at a speed of about 95 miles per hour.

The Fortune Cookie

I recently opened a fortune cookie and found the troubling message: "Your luck is about to change completely."

It kind of worried me, because I see myself as a rather fortunate person. The hidden "message behind the message" was that most people would see that folded fortune as a positive sign that things were about to grow better.

Where luck is concerned, most people probably believe just that—that things could be better. Through luck, we gauge our place in the world.

What possible reason is there for this kind of risk taking on our roads? The only explanation I can think of is that such hazardous drivers are actively testing their luck. When they arrive at their destinations, they are intoxicated with the feeling that they have looked at danger eye to eye and survived. The fact that they are endangering many innocent people in their absurd experiments doesn't seem to worry them. In fact, taking other people along on their insane journey adds to the intoxication of dancing on the edge of danger.

Many people flirt with danger in other ways that, while dangerous, do not threaten physical injury. For example, entrepreneurs flirt with risk when they start their new ventures—and that danger is part of the exhilaration of their lives. Will the fates smile on them and their new endeavor— or will the universe shoot them down?

Testing those waters is part of the game.

Testing our luck in these ways—just as in gambling—is a way to measure where we stand in relation to an apparently detached universe. If we are "lucky" (we win our bets, narrowly miss hitting another car on our drive home, or succeed in our businesses), we sense we are aligned with some invisible higher forces. If not, we feel we are "on the outs" with good fortune.

Luck and Superstition

An Italian-American friend of mine likes to tell stories about his superstitious Sicilian grandparents. "They had so many superstitions, we used to laugh behind their backs," he says. "Once I dreamed that one of my teeth had fallen out. When grandma heard, she insisted that my mother keep me home from school until the period of danger I was in passed by. Apparently, a dream about a lost tooth is one of the worst dreams in Sicilian folklore. There were many other superstitions, too, about having curses put on you. Then there were things that could be done—like giving money to a stranger's child—that were nearly guaranteed to trigger good luck."

In some cultures, finding a bird in your house is a sure sign that terrible things are about to occur. In others, dreaming about a stranger means you are about to find money. The list goes on and on.

I like to think of myself as a person ready for the twenty-first century. I like to portray myself as a modern man who lives above such antiquated beliefs and superstitions. Yet the truth is, I often get signs that I am perhaps not so modern after all.

A few weeks ago, I got one of those pesky chain letters in the mail. It put forth the usual spiel about how its chain had been unbroken, had traveled around the world four or five times. It told the story of a man who followed all the directions (added his name to the list at the bottom of the chain, and so on) then inherited a large sum of money from an uncle he did not even know. The letter also told about a man who did not follow the directions, then promptly broke his leg and saw his home go up in flames.

"Do not break the chain!" was the sobering admonition at the bottom of the letter.

Now, I did toss out the chain letter. I always do. But I have to own up that it made me worry. What if there was some truth to it? What if something bad really would happen to me because I had failed to send the letter along?

Of course, nothing bad happened. But the incident did remind me of the subtle psychological power luck holds over us. We think we're above it, but the specter of bad luck can give us pause.

Modern or not, luck still holds sway over us on some deep psychological level. It lies dormant on some hidden plateau of our psyche, waiting to emerge.

OUR CHANGING VIEW OF LUCK

As with chaos, the popular conception of luck has changed considerably over the course of centuries.

Luck, Visions, and Dreams

"I had a dream where I saw three numbers, so I went out and played them in the lottery," a woman once explained to me at a family party. Visions, dreams, and revelations have always been part of the belief systems that many people call "superstition."

Now, that woman might have dreamed of numbers many times, played them, and never won. But the point is, she won that time. And for her, that serves as confirmation enough in the efficacy of her visions.

In Old Testament times, people often drew lots to help them make decisions. By engaging in a random practice, people felt they could determine which of several choices God wanted them to make.

In the Middle Ages, churches and clerics became very concerned with the fact that people seemed to be gambling more and more often—in essence, obeying a false god. So the church classified gambling as evil and—even though gambling did not neatly fit into any previous category of sin—tried to end the practice. Perhaps church leaders believed that people were putting too little money into their tithes because they were gambling it away instead.

Then came the Enlightenment—the defining intellectual movement of the eighteenth century. Strongly influenced by the rise of modern science—and by the views of Bacon, Galileo, Descartes, Newton, and Locke, who lived in the preceding century—philosophers of the Enlightenment were committed to a new, rational view of the world. It was a view based on human understanding—finally free of superstition and religious dogma. These thinkers had a great deal to say about rationality—and, by extension, about common perceptions of luck and chance.

The principal philosophers of the Enlightenment included Diderot, Helvetius, Voltaire, and Hume. Rationalists to a man, they felt that human understanding could chase away superstition. Given time and careful inquiry, the human mind could reveal the real forces behind superstitious happenings and possibly religious experiences too.

The Enlightenment laid the philosophical groundwork for a way of thinking that we take nearly for granted today—the notion of probability theory. During the nineteenth century, it seems, mathematicians realized that luck could be understood and even controlled by mathematical analysis.

When you roll a single die, the chances are one in six that you will get a 1, a 2, or any of the other sides. When you roll two dies—or three, or four—the odds of obtaining a specific number become complex in a logarithmic progression. Yet the point is, those odds can be understood and predicted.

When a roulette player bets that an odd number will come up, she's making a two-to-one bet. If she wins that bet, she might increase the odds by betting on a column of numbers, which is a three-to-one bet. And so on. At every step, the gambler is taking a calculated risk of success or failure.

This kind of thinking is so widespread today that we are apt to lose sight of the fact that it was once quite revolutionary. To the average person only 400 or 500 years ago, the idea of a numerical relationship between chance and outcomes was simply not in the universe of human thinking. As with chaos theory, probability theory takes seemingly random events out of the realm of happenstance or superstition and ushers them into the realm of science.

Today, probability theory has gained widespread use in disciplines as diverse as stock market predictions and advanced computer design. With computers' abilities to digest and analyze vast amounts of data, it seems certain that boundaries of knowledge about luck will be pushed farther and farther ahead in the decades to come.

As with chaos, we may yet come to understand that luck does not really exist per se. Luck will be unmasked as a phantasm—a vanishing trick of human perception.

Authorities on Luck

Part of our preoccupation with luck has also become a preoccupation with authorities on luck—people who claim to be empowered to see into the future or recommend specific actions we can take to improve out luck.

"Somebody Is Going to Win!"

When I encounter someone who plays the lottery each week, I sometimes am bold enough to say, "Don't you know the odds of winning are ridiculously small? Why bother?" When I ask those questions, the response I hear most often is, "Well, somebody is going to win. Why not me?"

For such people, the computations of odds are beside the point. Within their own self-defined universe, someone is going to win. Why not them?

In its own way, this view of the lottery is just as valid and reality-based as that of a probability theorist with a supercomputer chugging at his side.

- Advertisements for "psychic hotlines" have become a fixture of late-night television advertising.

- Storefront psychics, tarot card readers, and the like can be found in many towns—and all cities—through the United States.

- Astrologers are not on the fringe of our society. In fact, almost all newspapers in America give space to horoscopes.

- Virtually all toy stores continue to stock Ouija boards. They've been a perennial seller for decades.

- History tells us that people who claim to see the future often take on significant power. Astrologers have become highly influential in societies as diverse as dynastic Egypt and modern-day India. The mystic monk Rasputin, for a time, held considerable influence over the Romanovs—Russia's last, great ruling dynasty.

Few people hold such psychological power over others as those who claim to see into the future.

While my wife and I were on vacation last year in the Czech Republic, we had dinner in a restaurant where a fortune-teller went from table to table, reading palms. As I have found at other times in such circumstances, many of the things she said seemed to come from some real body of knowledge about us. In other words, she seemed to "know things" about us.

I realize that such feats are usually tricks, in the most literal sense of the word. By making some assumptions, picking up on visual traits of people, and carefully couching their phrases, psychics are able to deceive people into believing that real psychic experience is taking place. When a psychic holds your hand and says earnestly, "You've been thinking about someone you haven't seen in a long time, someone who used to mean a lot to you"—well, very few of us are not moved or taken in.

At the time, I realized that I was allowing myself to be a little seduced. Yet wasn't it exciting, too, on some level? It was. Getting messages from "beyond" our normal range of experience always is, even when we know down deep we are being deceived.

Why Change Our View of Luck?

At this point in the chapter, you may be thinking, "This is all very interesting. But why should I even concern myself with luck when I've just read that luck is really a matter of my perceptions and the way I place value on life's events? If I can't control it, why worry about it?"

Those are very good questions, indeed. Like chaos, the events of luck really are beyond our control. I cannot change, nor can you, many of the events that life puts in our paths. We can, however, change the way we interpret those happenings.

I believe that we should change our relationship with luck for some very important reasons.

First, we will be more successful. When we see our relationship with luck in a newer, more objective way, we will loosen its hold on us. We will feel freer to try new things, even things that have less "chance" of success. Second, we might just be happier. Recognizing luck for what it is—an illusion, nearly a trick of the mind—is liberating.

Finally, we can regain control in many important areas of our lives. Freeing ourselves from the hold of luck empowers us to take responsibility for what happens in many areas of life where we might have previously felt hindered or stalled. When we realize, "*I'm* in charge of my life, not some unseen force," we free ourselves to act willfully and control more of the content of our lives.

HOW TO GET THE POWER OF LUCK WORKING FOR YOU

Feeling "Lucky" Adds to Success

Many statistics bear out the power of positive expectations. People who are "bulls" in the stock market statistically do better than "bears"—possibly because "bulls" feel courageous enough to invest more often. Similarly, successful entrepreneurs are people who feel lucky enough to press their luck and try new things.

When you see luck for what it is—a matter of perception—you free yourself from the yoke of inaction that might be called "feeling unlucky."

Now that we've unmasked luck for what it is—a filter or lens we have created to evaluate our relationship with the outer world—it might seem that the work of this chapter has been done. However, I think that we've only just begun. Because now we're going to see how to use our newfound image of what luck really is to consistently bring better things into our world.

Once we see what luck really is, we free ourselves to operate in life on a newer, higher plane. We needn't sit back and wait for lucky and unlucky periods or events. We need no longer feel our lives are at the mercy of unseen powers of good luck or bad—like those medieval fatalists who believed their lives were cyclical rides around and around a Wheel of Fortune.

Dumb Luck

Of all the references to luck in our culture—"lady luck," "lucky dog," and the rest—"dumb luck" is the most accurate.

Luck truly is dumb. It is a trick of perception. It cannot hurt us. When we see it for what it is—a chimera—it loses its power over us and we can lead better lives.

We are modern people and, armed with a broader vision of what good fortune is, we can begin to exert a new level of control over the content of our lives. How? What steps can we take? Let's take a closer look.

Have faith. A recent *Newsweek* poll found that 87 percent of Americans pray and *expect something to happen because of it.* It has always been clear to me that there is a direct connection between positive expectations—having faith—and receiving good things in our life.

People who believe that God or some higher power is working on their behalf really do experience better lives—perhaps even better "luck." The reasons for this might be mystical (a higher power really might be looking out for faithful people, even answering their prayers) or quite practical. After all, people who feel they are "in line" with a higher power really are more likely to try new things—to be adventurous.

And we know that, from a statistical point of view, more positive outcomes are more likely to result from simply trying more new things. If we never act, we have no odds of success. If we act greatly, our chances of good outcomes become great.

"God at My Side . . ."

"I credit the success of my business to my deep faith," a successful entrepreneur told me. "Each step I've taken, I've taken because I sensed God at my side." Perhaps God really was at his side. Or perhaps he accomplished more because he felt confident enough to try important things more often.

In the end, the question of whether this entrepreneur succeeded because he was faithful or because he tried more may be a moot one. The point is, he acted. His faith freed him to act, and he got the job done.

Develop a deep sense of appreciation for life. One of the most powerful ways to attract more positive things into your life is to develop, and practice, a deep appreciation for the positive things you have in your life. If ever you're down, if ever things are going against you and you think you can't get your good luck "working," start taking account of all the good around you.

When you take account of all the positives, you help yourself rise above the false perception that you are unlucky, or experiencing a period of bad luck. You encourage yourself to try new things—and as a result, more good things do flow your way.

I have often seen this principle at work with people whom I counsel. Often, when people experience a few setbacks in their lives, they lose perspective. Because of one or two setbacks, they start to believe that everything in their lives is going downhill.

The Luckiest Man in the World

An old friend called me last year to tell me he and his wife had just separated. "I'm the unluckiest man in the world," he said.

"How are your kids?" I asked.

"Great! Sally just graduated from Penn State," he said.

"How is your business going?" I asked.

"Great! We had a terrific year."

"And aren't you about to become a grandfather?" I asked.

"Yes, I am!" he said.

After a moment's pause, he added thoughtfully, "You know, Dick, I am still the luckiest man in the world."

Perspective is one of the best ways to change our luck—or, at the very least, our perception of it. Luck is perception, after all. So by changing our perception, we change our luck.

I always try to put things in perspective. Yes, a person might have lost a job. A marriage might have ended. A new disease might have appeared, one that requires adjustment and attention.

Yet when I point out the many positives that surround such problems, the result is always a brightening of mood. People who classified themselves as unlucky suddenly gain perspective. It takes only a few negative events, after all, to make us lose our perspective totally. An argument at home, a bad day at the office—and we believe our whole life is ruined. Everything is going downhill.

A high level of appreciation is the antidote—one that keeps good things coming and brightens our outlook at the same time.

Learn to get in flow. In the next chapter, we'll explore the topic of flow in great depth. In the flow state, you can accomplish prodigious things and reap wonderful rewards from many activities in your life.

In his book *Flow: The Psychology of Optimal Experience* (HarperCollins, 1991), Mihaly Csikszentmihalyi explains that people improve the content of their lives immeasurably when they learn to tap into the flow state and get it working for them. Be patient until the coming chapter, and you'll see how to use this remarkable state to get the "good things"—commonly known as good luck—flowing in your direction consistently.

Position yourself where good things are happening. There is no better approach than positioning yourself to increase the good things that come into your life—in other words, your "luck." You can exercise power to control the context of where you are and what you are doing.

I often tell the story of a man who loses his keys on a moonless night. A passerby comes along and finds him crouched down beneath a streetlight, searching.

"What are you looking for?" the passerby asks.

"My keys, I lost my keys," the man answers.

"Oh, I'll help you. Where did you lose them?"

"I lost them over there by my car."

"Why aren't you over there looking for them?" the passerby asks.

"Well, the light's over here," answers the man. "How am I going to see them over there in the dark?"

The message is, many of us are looking for good fortune in the wrong places.

It's like fishing. If your pond has no fish, you can have the best rod and reel and the finest casting technique that you can muster. But if there are no fish where you are, you're not going to catch any. You have to put yourself *in the way of luck*.

That might mean making different choices about who the people will be in your life, or where you live, or how you earn your livelihood.

We may have to change our patterns—as Stephen R. Covey teaches us in his book *The Seven Habits of Highly Effective People* (Fireside Books, 1990). Unless we make changes to put ourselves in good luck's way, we are unlikely to see our lives—or our luck—change.

Put more trust in your intuition. This may be a roundabout way of saying, "Have the courage to act more often, based on your intuitive insights." I believe strongly that our insights are not born "out of thin air." They well up from many small, unconscious messages we have received and stored up—until the point of readiness.

A Ripe Fruit Drops from the Tree

"I'd been experiencing terrible frictions with my teenage daughter for so long," a woman told me. "Then one day, I somehow recognized the moment when it was time to talk to her about the problems we'd been avoiding for so long. I opened up and started the discussion. My intuition was right. She was finally ready to tell me what had been troubling her."

Life and luck are often like that. We somehow know when it is time to act—and when the results are likely to be positive. By learning to heed those internal messages, we increase the chances of a "lucky" outcome. If we trust our inner voice, we often know it is time to act, just as surely as the ripe apple knows the moment to drop from the tree.

Carl Jung believed that we receive messages not just from our own unconscious, but from what he termed the "collective unconscious"—a deep well of knowledge and insight that is not ours alone, but shared by all people. When our intuition speaks and tells us to do something, the outcome will often be positive—or "lucky," in the common idiom we use to classify positive events and outcomes we don't fully understand.

Make choices. As with intuition, choices often present themselves as opportunities to claim positive outcomes and good luck. "I knew it was time to decide whether or not I would go back to get my masters degree," a man told me recently. "The time had come to decide."

The Would-Be Poet

A friend of mine spent her entire life saying that she was not quite ready to send out a book of poems she had written when she was 30 years old.

At age 40, she wanted to give it "one more look."

At 50, she felt it needed "a total revision."

At 60, she dismissed it as "just youthful scribblings" and started to write something new.

At age 72, she died and never sent out a book. She could never decide to do it. She failed to publish a single poem, and she was very unhappy.

It's possible that some publisher would have snapped up her book when she was only 30, and that more and more books would have followed. By failing to decide, she determined her own bad luck.

Without action, good luck is impossible. Through inaction, we seal our fate.

How can we take advantage of those pivotal moments to move our luck forward? The most simple, reliable way is to heed decisive moments—the times when we have to act—as opportunities to move our lives forward toward a more positive, fortunate place. And then, we must make decisions and act on them.

Be passionate about life. People who see themselves as "lucky" are often involved in pursuits that bring them real joy—about which they are passionate.

"I Hated That Teacher"

My friend Barry tells a remarkable story about passion's power to bring good luck:

"When I was in sixth grade I had a teacher who had made the entire school year miserable for me. I hated her. On the last day of class, after handing out ice pops to the entire class, she found she had three left over. So she devised a little game to decide who would get the leftover pops. She wrote a number between 1 and 100 on a slip of paper and put it on her desk. Anyone who could guess the number would win one of the extra pops.

"I won the first one. And she wrote a new number, repeating the challenge. I won the second pop. I then won the third. I disliked that woman so much, I wanted to get every last pop from her, and I think I was certain what each number would be.

"My friends were ecstatic and—no doubt about it—my teacher was absolutely spooked. My feelings must have been shining from my eyes. It was the happiest day of the year for me."

This story is a great example of the power of passion—even negative passion—to trigger remarkably lucky outcomes.

"I made a small fortune in commodities trading when I was just in my twenties," a man says. "I was totally involved in it, almost drunk with the experience. I could never have done so well otherwise."

Now, of course, gamblers feel that way too—and often they lose large sums of money. Yet the fact remains that when we try to accomplish things in areas of our passion, we tend to have better outcomes.

There are many reasons for this. We tend to be most passionate in areas where we are using most of our individual abilities. And we bring a heightened degree of attention, and more intelligence, to pursuits that excite us and spark our energy.

By identifying areas of passion and following through on them—like a miner who finds a vein of gold and chips it away through base rock to its very end—we live luckier and reap greater rewards.

Gather knowledge wherever you can. The more you know about things you are about to try, the better your chances are to achieve fortunate outcomes. Expert gamblers, for instance, win more consistently than neophytes. Stock traders who "know the ropes" are vastly more likely to avoid costly mistakes and do better with their investments.

The more knowledge you gain, the better your ability to "manipulate the odds" of whatever you attempt in life, by avoiding costly mistakes and miscues. "Beginner's luck" may be exciting. But it is less predictable, and ultimately less rewarding, than "expert's luck." Here are some pointers to remember:

- *Absorb, observe, and learn before you act.* Before you start a business, research how similar businesses have succeeded, and what their mistakes have been. The more knowledge you can gain, the slimmer your risk of failure.

- *Find ways to minimize the risk.* Evel Knievel, who jumped his motorcycle over piles of barrels and junked cars—even the Grand Canyon—liked to say that he was not really doing anything risky, because he had studied so much and learned to minimize his risks to an acceptable level. By analyzing every aspect of things you are about to try—risky things, especially—you come closer to ensuring a positive outcome.

Obsession with Luck

In my counseling work, I've had occasion to work with several compulsive gamblers.

One man's entire life was ruined by his obsession. He was addicted to the process of taking chances, and the money didn't seem to be the real issue. He owed bookies money, he owed everybody. His obsession had narrowed his life down to almost nothing. Every morning the man would wake up and begin thinking about the horses. He neglected his job. He neglected his friends and family.

In a sense, he was trying to control the world by controlling a private microcosm. The horse races were his whole life. If he could win at horses, somehow he thought he could win at life. Somehow, if he could just get the right formula, he could make his life right.

By trying to take control in such a limited way, the man had lost control of his life entirely.

- *Gather knowledge from people who've "been there."* Whether you're entering your first billiards tournament, driving a vintage race car, or cooking a complex meal for a large gathering of friends, talk to someone who has done the same thing already. The more knowledge you can gather, the greater your odds of a "lucky" outcome.

Take action. You can sit and think, "Boy, I wish my luck would change." But if you're not willing to do something to change your life, if you're not willing to take advantage of events around you and take risks, luck won't come your way.

Don't sit idly back and wait for good luck to come knocking. Go out and knock on the door of good luck. And if good luck doesn't answer, kick the door down!

I'm Glad I Live Here

Every year brings horrific news from different countries around the world. Recently many of us have exclaimed, "I'm so glad I don't live in Serbia! I'm so glad I live right here!"

There is a message hidden in those words, a message about luck.

The contexts of where we live goes very far toward determining our life experiences. It's easier to be lucky in a peaceful democracy than in a troubled, war-torn state. Similarly, it's easier to be lucky when we are surrounded by smart, cordial colleagues, a supportive family, or any other context that is positive and embracing.

The better the context, the better your experiences are likely to be. That's another way of saying, "the luckier" you'll be. To sway your luck, you may need to make some changes.

EXERCISES

1. **Ask yourself, "Am I lucky or unlucky?"** Answer as honestly as you can.

   What does your answer tell you—not about luck, but about your perception of luck?

   If you see yourself as lucky, try to discern why. Is it because of the positive things in your life? Because of good things that have happened to you? Great going! Try to capitalize on those feelings.

   If you see yourself as unlucky, try to get to the bottom of that feeling. What causes you to feel unlucky? If you look at the causes objectively, is there any reason you should allow them to color your enjoyment—*and the content*—of your life?

2. **Create a life inventory of "lucky" and "unlucky" events in your life.**

   When I tried this exercise, I saw that some of the events that seemed luckiest to me at the time they happened turned out to not be so lucky after all. That wonderful used convertible I was "lucky" enough to buy after I graduated college turned out to be a complete lemon. A "dream" job I landed turned out to be not so wonderful after all.

   By the same token, some events that seemed disastrously unlucky to me at the time have turned out to be among the best things that ever happened. The dissolution of my first marriage was a positive step. If it had not happened, I would never have met my present wife or experienced all the joys of a wonderful marriage. Certain career challenges that have confronted me seemed negative at the time—really "unlucky breaks"—yet they have paved the way for my growth.

By subjecting both lucky and unlucky events to later scrutiny, we are better able to see luck for the illusion that it is.

3. **Apply probability theory to a decision you are currently facing.** The exercise here is a simple one. Simply subject a potentially "risky" act you might consider and see just how far you can determine the lucky or unlucky outcome by analysis and careful planning. Here's an example of how this can work.

A woman I know believed she would have to be "terribly, terribly lucky" to start an Internet retail business—selling women's clothing—and have it succeed. But instead of relying on luck, she decided to try to control the possible outcome of her action by systematically reducing the level of risk.

First, she spent a few hours doing research on the Internet to see whether any other online businesses were offering the same kinds of products she was contemplating. The next day, she did some research on the start-up costs. The day after that, she phoned a group of friends and asked them whether they would be likely to buy clothing from the type of Internet business she had in mind. The day after that, she drafted a business plan.

Well, you're getting the idea. Step by step, this entrepreneur whittled down the odds of failure to the point where they became acceptable in her mind. "Luck will be a factor in whether or not I succeed, of course," she told me. "Yet I was able to reduce the odds of failure to the point where I became confident that the venture was at least worth a try."

4. **Play a game of poker.** Invite some friends over to your home, or ask family members to take part. Place small bets—a penny game will do. Notice your emotions as you play, and observe your thought processes. If you win two hands in a row, do you feel lucky? If you lose several, do you think your luck has soured?

As you play, try to remind yourself that these are tricks of perception and interpretation. There is no way your luck is increasing or decreasing, even though you may feel that way. You are simply observing the way your mind seeks to understand and codify random events.

5. **Open, read (and eat) five or six fortune cookies.** Try to be passive and observant. Just read them to yourself and see how they make you feel.

Do the positive messages make you feel expectant—that you are about to be lucky or actually see one of the cookies' predictions come to pass? In a low-level way, the cookies are weaving their spell on you. Just how do you react?

3 GET IN FLOW

The tango masters step out onto a brightly lit stage from the darkness of the wings. As the first notes of music sound, they are already immersed in the structure of the dance, honed and refined through hours of rehearsal over the previous weeks.

A moment later, something unexpected occurs. The man, for the first time ever, adds a tiny nuance to the dance. With his eyes locked on the woman's, he shoots her a drop-lidded, languorous smile. She mirrors that action back at him, adding a suggestive pout of her lip that sends a murmur of appreciation through the crowd. Then, a moment later, she interpolates something new of her own—an almost imperceptible roll of her right shoulder—which he mimics back to her.

These nuances arise as unexpectedly to the dancers as they do to the crowd. They are epiphenomenal embellishments that bubble up through a complex matrix of music, the structured dance they've practiced, and the many rules of the tango they have internalized over years devoted to perfecting their art.

As the dance ends, the spectators applaud loudly, but immediately quiet down. There is another couple waiting in the wings, and the audience wants the contest to continue. There is nothing quite so exciting, after all, as watching people who have entered into the "higher" zone of human experience known as flow.

When people think of the word "flow," they are apt to conjure up passive images. "I think of flow as, well, kind of drifting downstream, seeing what comes to me," a friend of mine reports. "I'm not making too many decisions yet about what kind of job to look for," says an accountant who just lost his job. "I'm going to go with the flow and just see what comes my way."

Yet when we probe a bit deeper, we find that many people recognize another, more significant kind of flow—one that they encountered on the job or while performing some routine task. "Everything just fell into place with that report I had to write at work today," an executive tells her husband at the end of a workday. "My report seemed to write itself."

"I really got lost in the process of raking my backyard," a retired man says with a self-deprecating laugh. "It was getting dark out there, but I really got into it, and I lost track of time." His spouse is hard-pressed to understand why he was out there alone in the dark, and why he came in so late to a waiting dinner.

WHEN FLOW COMES KNOCKING

Such statements close in on our understanding of the essence of flow—which, for many of us, remains a rather mysterious state that we cannot initiate on our own. We recognize the flow state when we are in it, yet believe that we cannot initiate it ourselves. We believe we have to wait passively until it comes knocking on our "mental doors," inviting us to enter and take part in some kind of altered reality.

Yet we also know that when flow does come knocking, we find ourselves in a wonderful, exciting new place. For many of us, flow is made up of the following aspects.

A sense of enchantment. One thing we can agree upon—those of us who have experienced the flow state, in any case—is that being in flow is truly a wonderful experience. In *Flow: The Psychology of Optimal Experience,* Mihaly Csikszentmihalyi defines flow as "a state of involved enchantment that lies between boredom and anxiety." That's as good a definition of flow as any I have heard.

A diminished sense of time passing. In flow, we often lose track of time. A lengthy car trip seems to fly by. The last 20 pages of a novel seem to speed by as we watch rapt, in a state of near-suspended animation.

A heightened feeling of connection to whatever activity is being done. Whether the person in flow is playing a sport, performing music, or driving a race car, there is a feeling of unity with the task at hand. At times, it can even feel as though the boundaries between that task and the person performing it have blurred. "Sometimes I don't know just where the piano ends and I begin," a touring concert pianist told a radio interviewer. This "crossing over into the process" seems to occur often in people who regularly get in flow.

A sensation that difficult things are being accomplished with ease. People in the flow state write novels, play piano concertos, win tennis championships, make love, and possibly even die. Think of another state that can lay claim to such credentials? Flow seems reserved for remarkable things.

An ability to exceed personal expectations and definitions. An opera singer comes from the stage, reporting she had no idea she could sing *Aida* so well. She achieved something unexpected and new out there on stage. Or a basketball team wins a game with a level of skill that exceeds anything it has achieved in previous games or practice sessions. In the flow state, we raise the bar. We set new personal benchmarks and standards for what we can accomplish in the rest of our lives.

Flow or Fun?

According to Mihaly Csikszentmihalyi, author of *Flow: The Psychology of Optimal Experience* (HarperCollins, 1991), flow is not the same as fun or pure joy.

Fun and joy can take place anywhere—upon meeting an old friend, asking someone out for a date and getting a yes, or taking a warm shower. Flow, in contrast, takes place during some type of active application—often, while pursuing a goal. Typically, it begins when rather stringent rules are in place.

Flow occurs while playing a game, for instance. Or flow can even become the game. Some people relate that they get into flow when taking standardized tests, like the SATs or GMATs. That's just one case where flow can erupt in contexts that are extremely rule-intensive.

An eerie sense of effortless control. A writer I know tells me that when he gets in flow, he seems to be directing a larger process. "It's almost like the words are coming from somewhere, not me," he reports, "and my real job has become to direct them, choose among them, and playfully nudge the process along. It's no wonder that the ancient

Greeks invoked their muses before writing or singing. In flow, something does come to visit you from some divine place that is not inside you. It is a little scary, but reassuring at the same time."

Lack of performance anxiety. In the flow state, there seems to be a total lack of self-consciousness and apprehension surrounding that age-old question, "How am I doing?" Of course, performance concerns can coexist with flow, as when a basketball team that is five points behind in the final minutes of the game suddenly starts pumping in baskets with Gatling gun speed. Yet even in such circumstances, there is apt to be such immersion in the process that all sense of individual ego falls by the wayside.

An absence of boredom. Perhaps this seems like a minor point to make, in light of the weightiness of the others I've noted above. But the fact is, flow has the power to banish boredom—not just from the activity in which it occurs, but from other events that surround it through the day. Perhaps this explains why creative people seem energized and excited by the most mundane tasks that fill the portions of the day when they are not working. They have spent part of the day in flow—and the excitement and energy is lapping over and infusing the rest of their day with new energy and excitement.

FLOW AND RULES HAPPILY COEXIST

Contrary to the common impression that flow is a passive state, flow is actually more likely to occur when we are operating in the presence of rules—often, a great many rules. Consider this random selection of situations where flow is likely to occur, and you will see that they all represent contexts that are pervaded by rules and restrictions.

Rules Help Flow

When you are in flow, you are entering a rule-based environment. You're concentrating on what is possible or not possible within the context of complex strictures and rules. Sometimes, these rules are not apparent to observers.

While writing his book about Alberto Giacometti, author James Lord spent four or five weeks watching the artist at work on a portrait. As the subject of the portrait modeled, Lord reports, Giacometti seemed to be moving ahead according to some complex internal set of criteria. Over the course of each five- or six-hour setting, Giacometti would make constant changes and revisions. Often, he would discard his previous efforts and start afresh.

Lord observes that Giacometti seemed to be in a state of total immersion in his work—walking some kind of patterned course.

A woodworker is engaged in cutting the pieces for an oak table. At the moment, he is cutting the mortises and tenons that will allow the crosspieces to fit precisely together for the table's legs. It is a process that requires complex measurements and meticulous cutting techniques. Yet in the midst of adjusting his power tools to close tolerances, the woodworker enjoys a keen sense of flow.

The New York Philharmonic is midway through Mendelssohn's *Scottish Symphony*. The conductor is working from the printed score. She can't change a note. None of the players can interpolate an extra note or make a tempo change, since they are all moving ahead in tight synchronicity. But—no question—they are all in the moment and completely in flow.

Flow and the "Renaissance" Human

Michelangelo was a master painter, a phenomenal sculptor, and an extraordinary poet as well. Ignacy Jan Paderewski was not only a remarkable composer and one of the greatest pianists of our century, he was also prime minister of Poland and a signer of the Treaty of Versailles that ended World War I.

We all know other Renaissance people, too—actors who are also good painters, violinists who are fine woodworkers, writers who excel at contract bridge or competitive chess. Could it be that the ability to enter the flow state in one competence opens the doors to flow in other areas too? It's a question that merits study.

A world-class figure skater is competing in the Olympics. To win a medal, the skater's performance must meet extremely stringent criteria. She must land the prescribed jumps or lose the technical merit points she needs to place among the winners. Yet again, despite the rules and strictures, she is in a state of flow that lifts her out of competence into the realm of art.

Clearing Brush

I have to admit that I also have an activity that brings me totally into a state of flow. People kid me about it, because it has little to do with high art or creativity.

My activity? Clearing brush in the country. Of the six acres I own, I have probably cleared one or two acres to date. On first blush, people might see me out there clearing brush hour after hour and say, "It seems so mindless. Why doesn't he hire someone else to do it?"

But it's an activity I really like, and I find it to be not so mindless at all. It is like participating in an evolving structure. I cut and I cut, then I pile up the branches. I see how many I have accumulated.

Is there enough yet to burn? How much have I produced in one day? If I decide to make a fire, how long will it take to burn? Is there enough time to get that done before I must go in for dinner, or should I wait and do my burning tomorrow?

I also consider the aesthetics of what I am doing. There is a lot of brush all around my house, and what I decide to clear away will exert a strong effect on both the appearance of my house and on the way I enjoy the outdoor space around it. Of course, while I am cutting, I do a lot of thinking. It is good physical activity. And somehow, I feel no anxiety about how much I have to get done on any one day. There will always be more to do, more progress to make, more to cut.

I Like Clearing Brush

I like the physical movement. It cleans up a messy part of my world. It makes a small part of the world more beautiful. It creates the context of a sanctuary. And it molds the natural realm around my house. There is some contentment about it. It comes from a controlling of consciousness: making something happen.

It's a very interesting state of mind, and very freeing. I create a structure and live through it, even though the rules are really not imposed from without. They evolve in the interplay between me and the process.

The Machinist and Flow

"When I was in high school, I demonstrated good skill as a machinist," recalls a man I know. "My metal shop teacher was so impressed by my skills that he got me a job in a machine shop—a job I held for several years. My job was to produce little cylindrical filters—just one part of a larger machine. I made tens of thousands of them over those years, just following the same repetitive steps and operating the same machines. I'd take a flat sheet of screen, cut it into little squares, put those squares through a roller to make cylinders, then weld the cylinders shut. I did it over and over again.

"I found it repetitive, but not dull. Each day, I knew just where I stood with the batch I was working on and which machine I'd use first. When I was alone in the shop, I'd often lose track of time. I'd hear the music on the radio with extraordinary clarity. Sometimes, time would seem to stand still. The complex process I was performing was strongly based in reality and rules, yet curiously it was mentally liberating."

DEADLINES, GOALS, AND DREAMS

We expect flow to occur most easily when we have no pressure or deadline to conform to—when we can just go away and be by ourselves. In fact, the opposite often occurs. We get in flow because of deadlines. Perhaps we even need the pressure.

"Without deadlines, I'd never get any quality work done," a journalist told me. "I need to feel the heat to get my juices flowing."

An executive voices similar sentiments: "When I get a whole team of people together to work on a problem and the stakes are high and time is short—well, then I feel like I'm really alive."

Goals, too, might seem to be anathema to the flow state on first glance. Yet goals often contribute to flow. "I spent several years taking classes to be a good amateur cabaret singer," a friend of mine reported. "I worked on my voice, concentrated on developing an individual style, developed my timing, posture, and the rest—and then the evening finally came when I was in a showcase. I went out on stage and—for me, anyway—something magical happened. It was the culmination of everything I had been dreaming about for years." Through her goals, my friend was trying to make her dreams come true.

Making our dreams come true, I think, is significant. Flow may be the most powerful tool we are given to make it all happen.

Skill Opens the Flow Doors

In the presence of complexities and rules, another characteristic of the flow state seems to logically emerge: *Flow cannot occur unless there is mastery.* It is really through the mastery of complex skills that we empower ourselves to move into the flow state. In fact, flow rarely occurs unless some degree of personal mastery is also present.

A professional magazine writer reports that, in midcareer, he is finally able to write stories to the exact length on the first try. "Up until last year," he says, "I always wrote my stories about 20 percent too long and needed to cut them. I finally have become able to write a good story to length on the first try—a skill it took me more than ten years to master."

Why is this ability allied to flow? The writer explains, "This new level of skill has unleashed a new level of flow. I can kind of play with a story as though it is a rising mound of bread dough, molding and shaping it almost unconsciously, feeling its internal heft and making constant decisions as I go along. I never knew this was possible, and it is a new level of immersion in the process."

The Process Itself Brings Joy

My brush clearing and the flow it brings cause me to feel joy—even though the activity seems free-form, almost unstructured. I know of other people who experience flow simply for its own sake.

In the small town where I live—in Westchester County, north of New York City—there is a man who regularly walks all the roads in the area. He's a hale man in his sixties, well dressed and energetic, and he simply walks around. When a local newspaper interviewed him, he explained that he just is a retired executive who likes to walk and rewalk the complex matrix of streets in the area. People see him, and he sees them and gets to know their faces. He also said that he makes a habit of picking up trash as he goes, and that he perceives patterns in what he gathers and finds trash interesting.

Another man I know has a metal detector and enjoys traversing an open stretch of beach in a highly organized way—one little slice of beach at a time. "People think I'm doing this for quarters, and that I find only bottle caps," he says. "But I find interesting things—old coins and pieces of jewelry that are intriguing, even if they may not be valuable. It's really the process that attracts me, as much as anything else. There's the wind, the sound of the surf, the process of dividing an abstract piece of land into a well-defined structure."

Driving, to me, seems to be a similar flow-inducing state. Surrounded by rules and laws and the necessity of controlling a car—a very complex mechanical device—we are often able to enter into a higher state of awareness as we move past new sights and into new vistas.

The tango dancers described at the outset of this chapter have achieved the ability to enter into flow by mastering an art form that is bounded on all sides by complex rules and traditions. Only by meticulous mastery of all these rules—and lengthy study under masters—have they built a skill foundation that enables them to transcend those rules and enter into flow.

Perhaps the message in these observations is that it is highly rewarding to study and work to gain access to flow in your chosen work, or in activities you love. By adding skills and aptitudes, you pave your way to a higher state of mastery. New, unexpected vistas will unfold.

The Pot Smoker and the Piano

"Back in the 1960s when I was in college, I shared an apartment with six other students," a friend of mine recalls. "I had a roommate who was a terrible pot-head. One day, much to our surprise, he rented a piano. It suddenly showed up in our living room.

"Each afternoon, our roommate would sit down at the piano, begin smoking pot, and try to play the piano. When he couldn't play, he smoked more pot. When we asked him what he was doing, he said, 'It makes sense. Knowing how to play the piano is in my head, if I can unlock it.'

"When we told him it might not work, he retorted, 'I'll show you!'

"Then, one day, the piano disappeared. Our roommate had called the music store where he had rented it and returned it. When we asked him what happened, he responded, 'I don't know. There was something to that thing I just couldn't get.'"

CHAPTER THREE

My friend's roommate had encountered an important principle. Flow cannot precede skill. It has to be the other way around.

Undaunted, my friend's roommate took up painting.

A Society of Instant Flow

People have often noted America's "culture of instant gratification." I think we are also part of a society of "instant flow." Time and time again we are attracted to products and activities that are designed to impart a sense of immediate—and unearned—mastery.

Some weeks ago on a subway platform in New York City, I heard a street musician at the other end of the platform playing rock music. He sounded pretty good, so I decided to walk the length of the station to see him play. When I got there, I discovered he had only two fingers on the keyboard. All the rhythm, harmony, and musical nuance of his performance came from the microchips in his battery-powered instrument. Yet he swung and swayed as though he were in a state of flow achieved by someone who had devoted years to musical competence.

In a video arcade, I saw an electronic game with a joystick that allowed the user, for 50 cents a play, to coordinate the movements of a very adept martial artist whose tumbling, kicking image fought another opponent on the screen. It was a chimeric likeness of flow and mastery that was cut off from the years of practice and self-exploration that any real-life martial artist must pass through to get into flow.

Interestingly, such "false flow" experiences have little staying power. They lose their fascination quickly as the player moves on to other, newer experiences. Real flow, in contrast, sticks with you. Pianist Vladimir Horowitz was still reaching new vistas in his artistry when he died, well into his eighties. And Morihei Ueshiba, founder of the martial art of Aikido, was still agile and able to evade multiple attackers when he died in 1969, at the age of 86.

Given the choice of flow that is either instant or hard-earned, I'd urge all of us to choose the latter. It hinges on hard work and mastery, but it has the power to lift up and enlighten our lives.

FLOW AND SELF-REALIZATION

Another remarkable aspect of flow is its ability to teach. Through flow, we build upon our knowledge of who we are and what we can accomplish. All the skills that have come from hard work and practice suddenly take on significance and meaning. By adding flow to those skills, we arrive at new self-definitions.

After entering the flow state for years in his business, an entrepreneur suddenly concludes, "Yes, I really do have what it takes for this, a special talent." He's made enough deals and survived enough company crises. He has finally found "his wings" and experiences a new sense of belonging. Or a student pianist finally feels "it" one day—the moment when flow appears as an epiphenomenon upon all her skills—and exclaims, "Well, maybe I do have what it takes after all."

Through the sense of self-actualization that comes with flow, we hammer out some kind of new creation that is ourselves—doggedly, slowly, brick by brick.

Some years ago, while visiting a sculpture park in South Carolina, I came around a corner and suddenly saw a remarkable statue called *Man Making Himself*. It presents a man, half turned around and half completed, who is carving himself from a block of stone. I see the flow experience as just that. It is a time when we literally create ourselves. It is the time when, even if briefly, we get to be the people we really want to be.

Prodigious Flow

When a musical prodigy only eight or ten years old suddenly captures the attention of the critics and music-going public, there is a sense of wonder at the youngster's skill. How could this newcomer have mastered such complex skills at so early an age?

Usually, the critics write comments like, "It is remarkable that this young artist is able to plumb the emotional depths of the Sibelius violin concerto." Yet I think that people are really wondering at something else too. They are wondering how a young person could have achieved an ability usually reserved for people of a far more advanced age—the ability to get in flow.

Part of the fascination of prodigies may hinge on just this internal conflict. A prodigy is not unlike a being with an adult's head on a child's body—a kind of divine anomaly. Over time, the public and critics intently watch the prodigy. Having achieved mastery at so young an age, will the youngster be able to keep it up? In fact, many prodigies are unable to do that.

Could it be that the gift of flow, imparted to prodigies so early as a nearly unnatural phenomenon, becomes too fleeting to recapture in later life? The answer to that question is not easy to find. Yet the connection between flow and prodigious talent is worth pondering.

FLOW AND HEIGHTENED EMOTIONALITY

The word "flow" seems to conjure up images of unpressured, easygoing activities. Yet often, flow occurs when the sense of urgency about the task at hand is very great.

John, an advertising executive, procrastinates whenever he has a big new-client presentation to make. He waits until the day is at hand, then whips himself into a state of near-frenzy and spends several very late nights in the office. Often, he inconveniences his staff and gets them as excited and upset as he is. When I talk to him about why he does this, he cites a number of reasons. "I'm disorganized," he says. Or "I have so much to do that I just can't make time for the big projects. They creep up on me."

Yet in the other areas of his work, he is highly detail-oriented and organized.

I believe—and I suspect John would agree with this statement, if I were to ask him—that he sets up heightened emotional circumstances around his most creative projects for a very specific reason. He needs to feel pressure, to feel a deadline close at hand, to focus completely on a task and get into flow.

Of course, there are healthier ways to get into flow than to panic, or cause panic in a group of other people. We can bring our whole attention to a problem, or follow the other steps we'll explore at the end of this chapter, to get flow going in a healthier, more positive way.

FLOW AS A STATE OF MIND

As a hockey player skates in to make a goal, her mind and body seem to be in a remarkable state of coordination. When a race car driver pilots his car around a curve at 130 miles per hour, he is in a rarefied zone indeed. His senses are relaying thousands of microbits of information constantly to his mind, which is making judgments and telegraphing back commands to his hands and feet just as quickly.

Performing Arts

Maria Callas, the great soprano, was famous for pitching fits during rehearsals. Many famous actors and actresses are also known for having volatile tempers.

On the surface of things, the actions of such people seem to stem from mere ego and the need to manipulate other people. But from another point of view, perhaps these artists are only trying to build the level of emotional tension they need to enter into flow.

Few of us ever enter such zones. Yet is extraordinary physical ability or robustness a prerequisite to flow? I don't believe so.

Not long ago, CBS's *60 Minutes* presented a story about a group of patients who were suffering from amyotrophic lateral sclerosis (ALS), also known as Lou Gehrig's disease. One man was almost totally incapacitated by the disease, but he was able to hold a paintbrush in his mouth and produce beautiful paintings. Another man, who was completely unable to move or speak, was able to type words by looking at a computer screen. He could still communicate with the world.

A reporter asked the second man, who had been vital and active only a year before, whether life was worth living on that basis. He reported that yes—life would always be worthwhile if he could communicate in some way. In a diminished way, perhaps he was in flow. And as long as that was not cut off—that ability to be part of a process and communicate—life was indeed worth living.

Flow on the Job

We associate flow with creative activities like painting and playing a musical instrument. Yet I'd wager that, from a statistical point of view, the number-one place that flow is experienced is at work.

Work, after all, is a context imbued with countless rules. It is a place where we develop skills and abilities over long periods of time. It is a place that imposes deadlines and goals, such as the need to finish a report or prepare a presentation. It is an arena where, by and large, creativity is valued and rewarded.

So why should it surprise us that we get in flow when preparing a report, polishing up a presentation, or tackling some other complex task? Why should it surprise us when we unexpectedly feel that a marketing report "seems to write itself" or a new-client presentation exceeds all expectations?

Why shouldn't we flow at work? What, after all, could be more natural?

HOW TO INVITE FLOW INTO YOUR LIFE

Now we get to the crux of this chapter—how not only to understand and appreciate flow for what it is, but also to make it a part of our regular experience. How, then, do we get in flow?

Getting Started

Procrastination takes us out of situations that might actually be flow experiences. So the first rule of getting in flow is: Don't shy away from things that need to be done.

I always hate to do my taxes. But once I get started, I like the process. I'm not a "numbers guy" at all. But to me, doing

taxes is like a big puzzle—a matrix of many rules and proce-
dures. I have to look for receipts, understand the forms,
transfer information from one line to another. It's very complex and I dread it all. Yet when I get started, I find the
process can help produce a flow state—an internal rhythm
that can be exciting, even fun.

My friend Christine, who dreads the many phone calls
she has to make on the job, reports a similar phenomenon. "I
have to call customers—ten or more of them each week—to
ask how pleased they are with our company's service. I dread
doing it. It seems like a terrible interruption in the rest of my
work. I tend to put it off.

"Getting started feels like wading into thick, gummy
molasses. Yet as soon as I've made the first call, something
happens. I get on a roll. I make one call and think, 'Well, that
was easy. I'll just make another one.' I get into what I term
my 'call mode.' A rhythm develops. Before I know it, I've
spent a productive hour and my weekly call quota is made."

The message is, action can open doors to flow. And curiously, flow seems likely to occur not only as we attack activities we love and long for. It can occur just as often when we
attack activities we see as distasteful. Once we begin, we feel
a sense of relief as we move the process along.

Athletes talk about being "in the zone."

Religious people talk about being "in ecstasy."

Artists talk about "inspiration."

They are all talking about flow.

I think there is a tie-in here with the personality types defined and identified in the Myers-Briggs Type Indicator® (published by Consulting Psychologists Press), commonly called MBTI or the Myers-Briggs test. This test indicates our preferred methods of interacting with the world.

- *Extroversion vs. introversion.* Extroverts are outgoing, motivated by people. At the opposite pole, introverts find energy in their own thoughts.

- *Sensing vs. intuition.* Sensing-oriented people take in information through facts. Intuition-oriented people digest information through its meaning and possibilities—even through fantasy.

- *Thinking vs. feeling.* Thinking people analyze information and use logic. Feeling people apply values and make subjective decisions.

- *Judging vs. perceiving.* Judging people are systematic, goal-oriented, and settled. Perceiving people are flexible, spontaneous, and open to change.

A central point of the Myers-Briggs test is that we often gain energy and grow, not by staying within our comfortable categories, but by moving toward the opposite polarities.

For example, a person who fears speaking in public often enters into flow when he tries it anyway and sees that he can carry it off. Or a person who is very goal-oriented from Monday to Friday decides to simply take a hike in the woods on Saturday, to let her thoughts go wherever they will—and suddenly finds her thoughts flowing to unexpected new areas.

The message is, try to move into new areas. If you find yourself putting something off, consider that it may well be a thing worth doing. Stretch into new areas and you will invite flow into your life.

CHAPTER THREE

The Importance of Concentration

Concentration is a remarkable ability of the mind—one that, I believe, is often undervalued. When you direct your mind concertedly toward an activity, you raise the process to a higher level and increase the likelihood that a state of flow will occur. Sometimes, you may even have to force yourself to direct your mind in this way. It can be a struggle.

Not long ago, for example, I had to read a book in preparation for a meeting I was about to attend. I delayed again and again, then finally decided, "Okay, enough putting it off. I have to do it."

I determined to do it in just one sitting. I sat down with the book and focused. I started out in a cursory way, reading the paragraph headings, finding the main points. Then, before I knew it, I really got going and a sense of flow carried me into the book with greater interest. In only two hours, I had done what I wanted to do. I finished the book and felt elated.

The Power of Concentration

If I really like to do something—playing the piano, preparing a meal according to one of my favorite recipes—I give my concentration willingly to it. If I'm doing something I don't relish, I have to force myself. That's the case when, for example, I have to paint a room or have a talk with a member of my staff whose work needs criticism or correction.

Yet I find that once I apply myself, the effect is often the same. As soon as I set my mind to the problem and really concentrate, I become immersed in the process. With luck, a sense of flow will visit me and I can move ahead with an uncanny sense of ease.

> **Flow on Ice**
>
> The skating rink is a great place to see the phenomenon of flow in action.
>
> Stand at the side of a rink where skaters are practicing their skills or dancing in pairs, and your eye will automatically drift toward certain skaters who have a particular sense of ease and magnetism.
>
> The skaters whom your eye identifies, more often than not, are those who have built their skills to the point that they are in flow. Flow gives them presence that makes them stand visibly apart from the crowd.

Directing your mind consciously at an activity—concentrating—can make all the difference.

Uninterrupted Time Is Essential

When I engage in my brush-clearing ritual at my country home, flow is much more likely to occur when I have uninterrupted time to devote to the activity.

On a day when friends are dropping by for lunch, or a contractor will visit to give me an estimate for some work to be done, my brush-clearing activity tends to remain on a level that feels fairly mundane and superficial. Such external constraints get in the way. In contrast, open, uncluttered time seems to allow the activity to soar.

When you have a special activity you're about to undertake and would like to increase the odds of getting in flow with it, I urge you to set aside some quiet time. Here's how.

- *Clear the calendar.* Some important tasks—planning that big report or presentation, for instance, or painting a landscape—require blocks of uninterrupted time. By setting aside an afternoon or even several days, you increase the chances of flow.

- *Be sure you have nothing scheduled and are unlikely to be interrupted.*

- *Get away from your doorbell and the phone.* Even the sound of your phone machine picking up calls in the distance can be enough to chase the flow state away. Let family members know that you would like not to be interrupted during the time you have set aside.

- *Find a place where you will not be distracted by other commitments.* A home office, interestingly, may not be a good place to enter into flow. Your filing cabinet, folders full of work-in-progress—all such things can provide too many distracting reminders of other activities you should be attacking.

Flow and Meaning

People are more likely to experience flow when the challenge they are facing has personal meaning.

I once read interviews that a researcher conducted with veterans of World War II. Some of their experiences tended to be very intense and rewarding—experiences in which the former soldiers recalled that they had felt a real sense of purpose and flow.

Interestingly, the difference between flow-inducing experiences and others often hinged on whether the veterans were involved in tasks they found to be personally meaningful. When guarding a gun installation, for example, they got more in flow when they knew they were protecting friends, not just guarding equipment for the equipment's sake.

- *Work in silence.* Don't play the radio. If the folks in the other room are playing music or watching the television, ask them to stop—or relocate to a silent setting. Silence invites the state of flow, and noisy distractions can frighten it away like a scared bird.

Time to Create

Yaddo is an artists' colony in Saratoga, New York, where artists spend their summer weeks writing, painting, and engaging in other creative work.

After breakfast, each artist-in-residence receives a box lunch to take to his or her studio in the woods. Artists are not permitted to visit each other during the day. A rule of silence is imposed on everyone.

In those uninterrupted, quiet-time blocks, creative activity takes place. It is a context intentionally created to increase the chances of flow.

If you are holding to a schedule, you have little chance to get the flow going. You will just be moving from one external demand to the next. Your internal process isn't going to have its true creative movement. Set time aside.

Setting Challenging Goals

For flow to occur, you need more than free time to "see what happens." You need a definite goal to motivate yourself strongly. Curiously, the presence of a goal may have more to do with triggering the flow state than the scope or profundity of the goal per se. The motivational force of a goal, in fact, seems not to hinge on its profundity. Here are some examples of simple goal statements.

- "I will outline the major sections of my new string quartet this afternoon," a composer declares. That orientation triggers flow and the work gets done.

- "I will cut out the pattern for the new dress I want to sew for my daughter's spring formal dance," a mother states. That, too, provides enough purpose to really get into flow.

- "I will take a few hours and hook up those new home theater speakers I bought yesterday," a man states. After a few pleasure-filled hours, the job is done and the man and his family are enjoying the rewards of his work.

- "I will practice pole vaulting every afternoon this week until I am able to break the state record consistently in practice," a high school track star plans. "Then, with those increased odds, perhaps I can break the record in the state finals next week." That personal goal gets the vaulter highly focused and in flow.

- "I will sit alone with the script of *Uncle Vanya* in a quiet place, let images play through my mind, and come up with a visualization of how my character will move across the stage in the scene we'll rehearse tomorrow," an actor plans. Alone with the playbook that afternoon, the actor sees the character take shape before his "mind's eye" and come to life through creative imagination.

The fact is, a wide variety of goals and challenges have the power to invoke the state of flow. They share few characteristics beyond these two: *The goal should be challenging. And it should mean something to you—whether it is composing a symphony or building a bookshelf.*

EXERCISES

1. **Take an inventory of times you have been in flow.** First think back to times when you have been completely immersed in a process—any kind of process, from raking the leaves to writing an article or playing the piano. For each flow state you can remember, write down its characteristics in the following areas:

   — *The context.* Were you indoors or outdoors? Was it day or evening? Were other people with you or were you alone?

   — *The physical activity.* Were you sitting at a desk or involved in vigorous physical exercise? Were you performing a repetitive physical task or doing something unstructured?

   — *The purpose or goal behind the activity.* Were you writing a report to meet a deadline or shuffling through creative ideas about how to write something? Were you swimming laps to get in shape or preparing your taxes?

   — *The level of pressure.* Were you just having fun with the project that got you into flow—or were you under the gun?

— *The skill base you brought to the flow situation.* Were you using a skill you had developed over a long period of time—such as dancing, playing a musical instrument, or shooting baskets? Or did some new activity get you into flow?

As you ask such questions about flow states you've experienced—you should be able to subject four or more to this analytical process—you may discern common threads. You may determine, for example, that quiet settings with a lot of goal-oriented pressure are most likely to move you into flow. Or you may determine that you move into flow when you are left alone to quietly play with ideas and creative alternatives.

You should also be able to identify your preferred type of context for flow—even create that context and apply it the next time you want to bring a powerful sense of flow to a problem or project you're facing. Do you get in flow when you're under pressure, for example, when you need to stand up before a group of people—or when you are by yourself, accountable to no one and nothing? Well, you can do those things again.

Understanding such factors can help you conjure up the flow state when you need it.

2. **Experiment with your skills.** Are you a skillful cook, a competent guitarist, a black belt in karate, or an effective public speaker? If so, invest some time polishing those skills—bringing them to a higher and higher state by taking a class, practicing diligently, or simply setting aside a block of time to become immersed in them.

In time, putting new weight on your areas of competence may lead to an ability to call up the flow state with greater reliability. You may even find that the sense of flow you develop in areas of competence can be applied to other areas of your life.

3. **Stretch into new areas.** If you don't think of yourself as artistic, take a class in figure drawing. Or if you believe you have little ability "with your hands," take a class in basic carpentry, home wiring, or auto mechanics. By stretching, you can open up new areas of energy and enthusiasm that can invest all your activities—old and new—with new flow and energy.

4. **Set some new goals, and get going on them.** A program of physical exercise, a plan to change careers, a determination to learn to speak a foreign language in a year—all such goals have an energizing effect that can help open the channels of flow.

   Instead of simply setting goals, try to make your work toward them a regular part of your weekly activity. If you're taking a class in French on Monday evenings, for example, find a French-language discussion or conversation group that meets at another time of the week. Or if you're studying a martial art, set aside an hour each week for solitary practice.

   When you work actively toward a goal, you invite flow into the process.

5. **Concentrate.** As suggested earlier in this chapter, applying concentration to a problem can yield surprising results—including an unexpected sense of energy and flow. Before undertaking an activity, make a personal commitment to concentrate on it and shut out interrupting thoughts or considerations. By consciously bringing your mind to bear on a problem or project, you raise the process to a higher level.

6. **Find a new context for activities where you would like flow to occur.** Ride your bicycle along an interesting new path instead of your usual route. Move your computer near a window so you can watch the trees and the birds as they come and go. Move your pottery wheel from a dark corner of your basement to a location where you can feel the breeze. Instead of reading and studying at home, go to the library and stake out a study desk in a quiet corner.

   A change of context can have a remarkable transforming influence on activities that are important to you, lifting them to new levels.

7. **Give yourself a deadline.** Instead of saying "I will learn to cook crepes," invite guests to a dinner party in two weeks, and plan to serve crepes at that time. Instead of daydreaming about finding an old wooden sailboat "someday," plan to find one by April, varnish it up, and get it in the water next summer.

   In making concrete plans, you'll gain energy and sense the beginnings of flow.

8. **Observe others who are in flow.** A basketball game, a chamber music concert, a ballet, or a circus all offer opportunities to observe other people who are masters at entering the flow state. With the right outlook and awareness, you can absorb some of their energy and impetus.

   Simply by being aware that *you are witnessing people who are in flow,* you can open your mind to its possibilities. In time, you can become a full participant in the rich harvest of life that this remarkable "other" state of mind makes available to us all.

4 MAKE DECISIONS

"The day Martha and I decided to get married was the day that changed my life for the better," says my friend Ross.

"Starting my own business was a decision that led to disaster," says my other friend Christine.

These two statements—seemingly opposed in terms of positive and negative, good and bad—embody the same central truth about decisions.

Decisions function as the turning points of our lives. Good decisions move us farther along the right path. Bad decisions move us along the wrong one. By making the right decisions, we shape our lives.

The quality of our decisions, more than anything else, determines the content of our lives. Decisions determine whether we will be:

Happy or unhappy

Fulfilled or unfulfilled

Accomplished or unrealized

Lonely or with other people

Materially rich or deprived

Adventurous or cautious

Significant in the lives of other people or negligible

DECIDE TO TRANSFORM YOUR LIFE

Decisions are the tools we use to create the lives we want. By making good decisions, we move our lives toward our goals and dreams. By making bad ones, we allow ourselves to fall victim to detours, mistakes, and wasted time.

Gaining a Sense of History

There is little doubt that decisions are moments not only of personal significance, but of historical significance as well. Here's a random sample of some decisions that have exerted a major historical effect in the last century:

Move Your Life Ahead with Decisions

When you take the bull by the horns and make decisions, you are taking control of destiny.

Will you marry or remain single? Have children or not? Pursue your real passion in your work or not? Take charge of your health through diet or exercise, or sit back and see what happens?

Our decisions are our destiny.

- Serbian nationalist Gavil Princip decided to shoot Archduke Ferdinand, triggering World War I.
- The United States, after wavering, decided to enter World War II.
- The United States decided to drop atomic bombs on Japan, killing hundreds of thousands of civilians and hastening the end of World War II.
- Dr. Martin Luther King chose to apply the principles of nonviolent protest to combat American segregation.
- President Lyndon Johnson decided not to seek reelection during the height of the war in Vietnam.

Then there are smaller decisions, which also changed the course of our century:

- Igor Stravinsky and Serge Diaghilev collaborated to create *The Rite of Spring*, a rhythmic and dissonant ballet celebrating pagan ritual.
- Henry Ford decided to mass-produce a car, the Model T.

Jeremy's Family

Jeremy came from a family in which, as he puts it, "nobody did much of anything. My parents didn't travel, didn't try new things, didn't believe they could ever become wealthy, experience excitement, or basically do anything at all. They lived in an uninteresting town, but said it was 'good enough for them.'

"Extraordinary things were for other people. It drove me so crazy that I began to 'adopt' my friends' families—their parents were reading books, trying out new options.

"I made a decision to break out, because I felt stifled, and that resolution changed my life. Without it, I would have condemned myself to a miserable existence."

- Pablo Picasso, thwarted by the limitations of classical painting, expanded the horizons of the human form in works like *Les Demoiselles d'Avignon*.
- IBM decided to market a personal computer.

On it goes, with decisions transforming society and transforming lives too.

Without decisions, our lives—and society as a whole—would remain in stasis.

Avoiding the Common Pitfalls

What are the impediments to making these decisions and then acting on them? There are many, but these are among the most common.

Fear of the unknown. Many of us are caught in a "comfort trap." We may not be too happy in our lives, yet we fear the discomfort that might come as the result of trying to do something about it. We might experience a temporary loss of income if we changed jobs, for example. Or if we decided to get married and the marriage was unhappy, we'd be miserable.

People who succumb to such traps agree to stay stuck in ruts of their own creation. Their lives go nowhere.

Disharmony with personal or family perceptions. Many people who fail to act make statements like these: "Nobody in my family ever tried anything like that before. We're just not that kind of people." Or, just as common, "I was never very smart in school. I don't think I have what it takes to get into college."

Challenging and rewriting those scripts is often a necessary precursor to change.

Fear about "what people will say." One former executive summarizes this decision-making block quite succinctly: "My job was a disaster. I was stressed out, panicky, spending no time with my wife or kids. I dreamed about getting out of the rat race, maybe starting to teach. Yet despite the fact that my work was doing extensive damage to myself and my family, I asked myself, 'What will people say? What will my golf buddies think when I tell them I'm throwing over a big paycheck in favor of scaling back?' I was letting those imaginary conversations paralyze my life."

Changing that kind of thinking requires work. Yet as the man himself said, most dreaded conversations with judgmental people really turn out to be "imaginary." Ultimately, it is more important to remain true to ourselves and to our families than to anticipate the opinions of people who are only casual observers of what takes place in our lives.

Fear of failure. "What if I fail?" is another common cry of people who are afraid to move their lives forward. For them, it's safer to remain stuck than to risk anything new.

Often, this blockage disappears by simply creating a "worst-case scenario" for the decision you are contemplating. If you take time off for graduate school and it doesn't appeal to you, what would happen if you dropped out and moved back into the workforce? If you started a company and it didn't prove to be profitable, what's the worst thing that could happen to you?

Gina, the Class President

Gina, who is an accomplished executive today, had a turning point in her life.

"I was sitting at a table in our high school cafeteria," she recalls. "At the time, elections were being held for class officers. Two of my friends turned to me and said, 'Why don't you run? You'd win!'

"I said, 'Yeah, right! I could never win!' But I let them talk me into it and I won the election, against three opponents, on the first ballot.

"That decision to run, which was kind of forced on me, showed me that my self-definition was off base. A little bit at a time, over the years, it led me to try things I might not have tried otherwise. I think my two high school friends did a lot to help me change the course of my life."

Having the courage to confront such questions—to codify and understand the real pitfalls that might accompany any decision—you can become a victor over your fears, not a victim of inaction.

RECOGNIZE DECISIVE MOMENTS

In popular culture, decision making is often characterized as "making up your mind." We often hear phrases such as these:

> "He wanted to start a business, but he never did because he couldn't make up his mind."
>
> "She never did make up her mind about having children, and now it's too late."

In a sense, this common notion of decision making—that it is little more than overcoming mental laziness—is off base and distorted. Decisions are made not just in the mind, but through a complex interplay between the mind and forces in the outside world.

There is something very special and distinct about the act of making decisions. The times when we take action and decide often stand apart as significant events in our lives. We hear people summarize those moments with words like these:

> "Suddenly I knew what I had to do. It all became clear."
>
> "There was no time to be indecisive. I had to act."
>
> "It all kind of came together for me and it was clear what I had to do."

You've doubtless used similar statements to summarize the times in your life when you acted decisively—when you suddenly knew just what you had to do.

Reaching a Decision

A decision point is the moment when all the information we have inside and all our information from the outside world suddenly come into focus. We're in a state that is highly conscious. Our inner understanding of ourselves and our knowledge of the world come together in one attitude, one action, one decision.

Moments of decision making are among the most focused and most energized in the human experience. The ancient Greeks seemed to recognize the fact that decisions occupied a special place in the human psyche. This is why they had two words for time. *Chronos* was their word for chronological time—the minutes that follow minutes, days that follow days. *Chairos* was their expression for a special moment of decision—a time of heightened importance that stood above the flow of regular time.

Chairos might have been the moment when a general decided to cross a river and wage an attack, or the time when a hero suddenly realized that someone he had thought to be a friend was really an enemy and needed to be killed.

We see that such decisions are not made just "in the mind." They are the result of a complex interplay between the mind and the outer world. The mind digests and considers real-world information. Then finally, a moment of high awareness dawns and a decision is made. When that happens, we enter into a state that is similar to flow. Yet rather than becoming enchanted with a process, we become engrossed in an action or a goal. Our will is called to action. Suddenly, the path becomes clear.

CHAPTER FOUR

The Time Frame of Decisions

Sometimes, external events thrust a need for sudden decisiveness upon us. Because of external events, the time to act is now.

"I was in a car accident several years ago," my friend Jeanne recalls. "I had broken a few ribs and possibly my leg. Within minutes, I was in an ambulance. The medical technicians asked which hospital I wanted to be taken to, and gave me three options. I decided. From the moment I arrived in the emergency room, more quick decisions were needed. When it became clear that I'd need an operation, I had to decide whether to stay in that hospital or be transferred to another one nearer my home. I opted for the latter. I called my husband and we quickly decided to call my sister and ask her to pick up our kids at school. My husband called my physician and arranged for him to meet me when I arrived at the hospital near our home. Since I needed an operation quickly, we decided to go with my doctor's recommendation for an orthopedic surgeon instead of interviewing two or three.

"My husband and I made many more important decisions in six hours than we usually make in six months. It was a tough period, you can bet, but at the same time it was kind of elating to be moving ahead so quickly."

At other times, decisions proceed at a far slower pace.

"I'd been toying with the idea of going to seminary for years," Robert explains. "I gathered information, thought back on my career, and talked to my wife and kids about whether our finances could be juggled to allow me to take time off from work.

"Even when we decided it was a 'go,' we had more decisions to make. When was the best time to make the move? Which seminary would be right for me? It took a while to put all the pieces in place before I could take action on my decision."

It's interesting to note that, in both these cases, the decision makers are engaged in a similar process. They're gathering and digesting information and weighing it against desired outcomes and goals. In a medical emergency, there is no opportunity to evaluate alternatives and consider options at length. In a decision to make a career change, there is far less pressure. Yet the essential process is the same.

The Role of Information

Since the quality of our decisions is directly influenced by the quality of information we have to work with, it's obvious that decision quality improves with greater knowledge. The knowledge we need to make good decisions comes from many sources. Here are several that can make the difference in empowering us to decide and move our lives ahead.

Real-world knowledge. The more we know about the world, the more we see opportunities to make significant decisions. A woman who dreams about starting her own company, for instance, can move closer to making a life change in that direction by learning more about other women who have made the same move she is contemplating.

Valuable knowledge can be gained through education and degrees, of course. By studying journalism or electrical engineering in college, for instance, you begin to build a knowledge base that can empower you to make a sound, reality-based decision about what to do with your life.

Just as often—perhaps more often—the knowledge that is needed to make good decisions comes to us through living. When we are open to the messages of our own experience, we gain the insight we need to move our lives ahead.

Inner knowledge. All our self-reflections, experiences, and self-beliefs come to play in the decisions we make.

Information Drives a Decision

"For years, I'd been fascinated by the inner workings of the companies that employed me," a college professor recalls.

"I loved to watch how decisions were made. I loved to observe people in groups working together. I was fascinated by people in power and the way they used their positions.

"One day, I picked up a book and read that the author had a 'Ph.D. in organizational dynamics.' It was like a light bulb going on in my head! I had never heard of that degree. I suddenly knew that, if such a degree existed, there was an organized way to make a study of the same questions that were already occupying my mind. A pathway suddenly opened for me. I started to investigate graduate programs, got my own doctorate, and am now an academic as well as a consultant.

"One piece of knowledge opened the doors for me and showed me the way."

Self-knowledge may be harder to acquire than real-world knowledge. Some people engage in therapy for years to understand the kind of people they are, and what kinds of blocks they may be placing between themselves and their own happiness.

Other people are able to grow and adapt in response to the reality-checking messages the world is sending them. This process has been defined as learning by the "school of hard knocks." That school might not be an easy one to attend, but it often sends the very messages we need to make effective decisions.

Are you the right kind of person to make the decision you are contemplating—starting a business, becoming a par-

A Singer's Self-Knowledge

Jonathan, who studied to be an opera singer, had some important self-knowledge forced upon him.

"I was a pretty good singer," he recalls. "I went to a very good conservatory, I had a good voice and I was an excellent musician. But when I got into the real world, I started to mess up singing at auditions. I'd have a bad audition, and my self-image would spiral downhill like a roller-coaster.

"Then I happened to see Placido Domingo sing two performances of *La Forza Del Destino*, just four days apart. In the first performance, he had a terrible night. He cracked notes. He even had a memory lapse. In the same opera four days later, he sang like a god. He had been able to put the previous performance completely behind him.

"I realized that I didn't have the resilience it takes to be a singer. It was a very hard lesson, but in the end, a very good one that helped me decide to take my life in another direction entirely."

ent, going back to school? While it is a mistake to let self-limiting beliefs hold you back from taking action, it is equally unwise to move ahead intrepidly toward goals that do not reflect your true interests, abilities, and ambitions.

In my work as a pastoral and occupational counselor, I meet with many men and women who, at midlife point, are trying to undo decisions made long ago on the basis of incorrect or insufficient self-knowledge. I talk with lawyers who should never have become lawyers, people who waited too long to become parents and who are now in despair—the list can go on and on.

The point is, know yourself as best you can. When a decision presents itself, ask whether it is consistent with what other people see in you, and with your emotions. When real-world knowledge and self-knowledge fail to mesh, a bad decision is often the result.

DECISION-MAKING STYLES AND SKILLS

When it comes to making decisions, what is your style? Do you make decisions easily, even courageously, or do you hold back? Do you wait until you have amassed all the pertinent information you feel you need in order to make a good decision, or do you act quickly, despite a lack of evidence or fear of risk?

Letting the Arrow Fly

In his book *Zen in the Art of Archery* (Random House, 1989), Eugen Herrigel describes how a Zen archer releases the arrow from the bow. The arrow is placed on the string, drawn back, and then held ready. The archer does not consciously decide when to let the arrow fly. He waits until the arrow releases itself.

Some of the most effective decisions can be like that. We gather information and ponder issues; then suddenly the decision is released according to its own inner logic and maturation. We are not always the ones to say, "I am ready to decide." Sometimes, a decision speaks to us with such force that we become clear about it and act in accord with its energy.

As in the last chapter on flow, I think it can be helpful to consider some of the personality types presented in the Myers-Briggs Type Indicator® (MBTI).

Judging Versus Perceiving

We can gain some insights into our own decision-making styles and abilities by considering where we might fit between the two polarities of judging and perceiving.

Judging people (the J's) are systematic and goal-oriented in making decisions. Their decision-making strength lies in the ability to make decisions quite quickly, based on the knowledge and information at hand.

A J Makes Up His Mind

After college, the son of a friend of mine took the $4000 he had saved and went out to buy his first car. Since some of his parents' friends drove fairly expensive European cars, he used his savings to buy an ancient Mercedes. The first repair the car needed—pretty quickly—was so expensive that he had to borrow money from his parents to pay for it. Shortly afterward, he sold the car.

"I thought a Mercedes would be a great car," he explained, "but I didn't factor in the age of the thing."

This poor fellow—who now pilots a Toyota—made a quick and firm decision based on a limited supply of knowledge and experience. He made a "good" decision that turned out to be bad. That is often the fate of J's—who tend to base their decisions on one or two "firm" pieces of information that, when added up, do not quite total a whole.

The Encyclopedia Salesman Meets a J

A college student took a summer job selling encyclopedias. He knocked on a door one day and began his spiel to a man and his family.

After a few words, the man interrupted and said, "Wait a minute. An encyclopedia is a book, right?"

The salesman confirmed it.

"Well," the man said, "I read a book once and I didn't *like* it."

The salesman packed up and left, for there was no fighting such iron-clad logic. He had experienced, first hand, the decision-making power of a J.

The man showed him the door. That was a definite J person.

On the downside, their decision-making weaknesses often lie in their tendency to make decisions on the basis of little information that may—or may not—be the best.

Perceiving people (the P's) are better able to deal with fuzzy outcomes and uncertainty. They are able to gather information systematically, over time.

On the downside, they often wait for all information to be gathered before moving ahead. They often delay decisions unnecessarily—even indefininitely—while they make up their minds.

Honing Your Decision-Making Ability

What are the benefits of honing your decision-making abilities? There are many, but I'd like to highlight some of the most important ones here.

- *A life of accomplishments.* Making decisions is the surest way to move toward your goals. It's the most effective way to keep your ambitions from becoming "pipe dreams" that are never acted on or realized.

- *More adventure and momentum in your life.* When you gain the courage to make decisions and act on them, your life becomes more diverse and more energized. You might make more mistakes in your life, it is true. But as many successful people have observed, they had to make some of those mistakes on their way to realizing their full life potential.

- *An interesting life.* This may sound like "small potatoes" in light of the weight of the benefits I mention above. Yet is it, really? An interesting life is something we're all entitled to.

- *A more realized self.* Self-knowledge comes from trying and testing different things in our lives. By interacting with the world in a courageous way, we mature and grow deeper in our lives and our relationships.

- *A richer life.* The question "What would I like to be remembered for?" has by now become something of a cliche. But it is nonetheless worth asking.

Would you like to make a difference in the world and in the lives of others? Your ability to decide on what you would like to accomplish—and then take decisive steps to move ahead with that vision—is the greatest determinant for the richness and the importance of your life.

HOW TO BECOME A BETTER DECISION MAKER

If you're determined to reap the kinds of benefits outlined above, how should you get started? If you are already adept at decision making, how can you become even more adept, raising your proven ability to the level of a finely honed tool for personal progress? Let's take a look.

Acknowledge the complexity of decisions. Remember, "making up your mind" is not such an easy thing. Nor should it be, in many cases.

In my work as a psychotherapist, I often have clients who come in, describe a decision they are facing, and then say, "What should I do?" Sometimes they even ask pointedly, "So, should we get married?" or "Should I invest all that money in the stock market or not?" Of course, there is a lot

When J's and P's Collide

A friend of mine who is a classic P—very methodical in his decision-making style—was shopping for a car. After a lot of research, he decided to try out a Lexus and invited his wife to come along for the test drive.

He told her, "I'd just like to drive this car, and I think we ought to drive some other cars too. I'm not ready to make any decisions. If we like it, I want to research dealer costs and bargain for the best price."

He and his wife visited a Lexus dealer and, with the salesperson along for the ride, took a test drive. My friend and his wife both drove the Lexus. Then, on the way back to the dealership, she turned to the salesperson and said, "We'll take it."

And they did.

My friend was flabbergasted, but he has to admit that it has been a great car. His wife's J decision-making style resulted in a good decision, albeit one that took the wind out of his sails.

of precedent in our society for bringing such decisions to an open forum, whose ranks include Dear Abby, Dr. Joyce Brothers, and telephone psychics. But I always refrain from giving pointed advice. It is up to the person who is in conflict to decide and move ahead with the results.

Decision making, after all, is a complex, highly individual process. And it is not simple. For some pragmatic people, coming to a decision is a matter of making lists, analyzing outcomes, then deciding to act.

For more intuitive types, a decision may come only after a lengthy period of digesting, internalizing, and waiting for things to suddenly "click." Like the ancient Greeks, these people suddenly find that everything becomes clear and they enter into a heightened state of *Chairos*. It's almost as though the decision was there all along, waiting to be seized upon and validated before action could be taken.

A Nondecision Can Become a Decision

"I want to get married and have a family," says a woman I know. Yet she has spent years moving from one relationship to another, without settling down. And now she fears she has waited too long.

It's hard not to accept her explanation that she has not yet met the right partner—that she has had a series of relationships with the "wrong" men. Yet it might also be possible that she has delayed the act of decision making unnecessarily.

This is the kind of knowledge only she can have about herself. But it is further corroboration of the fact that when we fail to make a decision, we are really making a decision in disguise.

The point is, no one else can determine the decision-making style or process that is right for you. It's an area of your life where you truly call the shots. Your spouse, family, or business associates may wonder about your decision-making style, asking, "Why can't she make up her mind?" Or "How can he make such significant decisions on the basis of so little evidence?"

Your decision-making style is yours alone. Learn to enjoy it and relish it, resisting any suggestions that you are doing it wrong. Your decisions, like your life, are up to you.

Depressurize the decision-making process. Replace the idea of "good or bad" decisions with the concept of decisions that move you forward toward your destiny—or impede that movement. If you can depressurize decision making in this way, you can see decisions not as doors that will either open or shut, but as part of an ongoing, playful process of moving forward with your life. Try to remember that "mistakes" in life are really very few. Mistakes are only opportunities to deepen our insight, gather information, and find more effective ways of living.

Don't justify your decisions to anyone but yourself. Yes, your spouse, children, or friends may be asking pointed questions about choices you have made in your life:

> "How could you leave a profession that was paying you such a good living wage?"
>
> "How could you buy a simple, modest home when you could have the means to afford something more lavish?"
>
> "How could you allow your son to take two years off before starting college, putting him 'behind' his friends on the fast track of life?"

Every decision you make in life is open to interpretation—sometimes, outright criticism—from other people. Trying to anticipate this picking-apart process can lead to serious consequences. You can decide to refrain from making decisions that you fear will be misunderstood by others. Worse, you can "water down" your decisions setting aside the choices you envision in favor of ones you believe will be better accepted by other people.

It takes courage, yet the fact is that we need to take responsibility for our own decisions and actions. Whether other people understand or misunderstand what we do is a secondary consideration. The primary issue is our ability to make up our minds and act, based on our own internal logic and processes.

Know yourself very well. This piece of advice sounds a bit daunting. And it is. Yet the more you know about yourself, your desires and wishes, the better able you become to make decisions that are right for you.

Are you a J or a P, for instance? Do you rely more on judgmental thought processes or "softer" perceptions? Do you hesitate before making life's bigger decisions, or do you act with assurance? Have you made decisions in the past that you regard as negative, and do you balk at making similar "mistakes" again?

There are no easy ways to gather this kind of information. Many people engage in psychotherapy for years in an effort to find out. Yet there are other ways to gain the kind of self-knowledge you need to act decisively.

I recommend a regular process of self-inquiry, such as meditation or prayer each day. Another good choice is to keep a journal, writing each day about your thoughts, goals, problems and current life challenges. Any process or routine that puts you in closer touch with yourself helps build a body of self-knowledge that—sometimes on a subconscious level—comes to your aid when choices must be made in your life.

Develop a curious outlook toward the world. Every piece of knowledge you gain—from far-flung sources if need be—can help build the kind of knowledge base that leads to better decisions.

I drive some of my friends a little crazy with my curious attitude toward life. I meet someone at a party and want to know everything about him—where he's from, what it was like to grow up there, what kind of work he does, why he finds it interesting. When I first encountered the Internet, I wanted to know all about how it works.

I'm also very curious about all things musical, and I've spent years learning about pianos. I drop into piano show-rooms; I talk to pianists. Because I am a pianist, I've tried out dozens of different pianos, probably hundreds. In the last few months, I've decided to buy a new piano, and I find that the knowledge I've gained through simple curiosity is really valuable in making a decision about what to buy.

Knowledge Paves the Way to Change

If you decide to become a professional musician, you have to know how the music world works in order to succeed.

If you want to become rich on the stock market, you need the technical expertise to invest wisely.

Many things in life are possible—most things, in fact—if you are willing to gather the broad-based knowledge you need to make informed decisions.

Over time, a curious outlook can be your best tool in making good decisions. I think it leads to better decisions than conducting sudden, last-minute research into a problem or enigma you're facing. Deeper knowledge, acquired over years, allows your decision-making engine to "fire on all cylinders" to make connections and judgments that you could not otherwise have achieved.

Refrain from thinking in catastrophic terms. Many people, faced with decisions, immediately envision the worst of all possible outcomes.

"If I start a new business and I fail, my family will be in financial ruin," one man says. "I have diabetes and if I start to exercise, I'll just throw my medication routine hopelessly out of balance," says a woman who puts off starting an exercise routine.

Develop a Jeopardy Mindset

A woman stands on the set of the *Jeopardy* quiz show. She's made it to the final round.

The question is, "What is *sic semper tyrannis*?"

She happens to know that those were the words shouted by John Wilkes Booth after he shot Abraham Lincoln. Knowing that wins her a new Oldsmobile. Then, when she can translate the words ("thus be it ever to tyrants") she also wins a trip to Hawaii.

The message is that small bits of seemingly inconsequential knowledge can lead you to deeper awareness. Gather all the knowledge you can—even little bits that seem useless.

It is far healthier, I think, to construct a worst-case scenario for decisions you are contemplating. Ask "What is the worst thing that can happen if I try this?"

Interestingly, the answers to that question often provide the clues to better decision making. If you fear that your family will experience financial hardship when you start a new business venture, for example, perhaps you can surround your new venture with some good financial planning that would remedy those problems before they even occur. If you fear that an exercise program will have negative repercussions on a medical condition, you could talk to your physician and make careful plans about starting off slowly in your exercise instead of deciding, "No way. Can't do."

Succumbing to half-realized, unfocused fears is a certain way to stop deciding and stop moving ahead with your life.

Seek the advice of loved ones and close friends. Have the courage to ask "significant others" about what they think about you and where your life is heading. (It takes courage, and a lot of it!) Trustworthy people can often provide needed clues to the kinds of decisions you should be making.

"You're so miserable in your work" was an alarming statement that a friend of mine heard from his wife when he asked for some career advice. That input led him to see that she was right—he really was miserable in his work. Her words served as a needed catalyst for overdue change.

"You're too hung up on money," a woman was told by a friend. "Don't you know you've already established a lot of financial security and you can start to enjoy your life a little bit more?" Those words encouraged the woman to take a two-week vacation in the Greek islands instead of settling for long weekends all summer long so she would not distance herself from her office and her work.

Overcoming Your Background

The world is full of people who overcame extremely disadvantageous circumstances—poverty, broken families, and more—to reach real success.

Thomas Edison is a fine example. So is Abraham Lincoln. Such people don't accept the idea that they are doomed by their circumstances. They exercise their right to decide to move beyond, move out, and live exceptional lives.

Are you stuck somewhere in a belief system that tells you, "You can't do it—not from where you come from"? If you are, you are almost certainly selling your life short. You can do otherwise. All you have to do is decide.

Be aware of all your decision-making options. Obviously, not all decisions require immediate action. There are often other options.

- *Delayed-action decisions.* If you decide to leave your job and attend graduate school, you are under no obligation to quit your job tomorrow if you make that decision today. You can make that kind of decision now and put the pieces in place gradually over time by investigating different schools, saving the money you'll need, setting up a financial plan with your spouse, and taking all the other preparatory steps required. A decision—even a fairly impulsive one— does not always demand impulsive actions.

- *Provisional decisions.* You might make your decision to start a software development company contingent on first determining some very specific facts. Are other companies already marketing a software program similar to the one you have in mind, for example? What are the start-up fees for the kind of venture you have in mind? What will the legal fees be to copyright your new product? How much will marketing cost? Such decisions start with a line of thinking that says, "I will do such and such if I can first establish the following." Such a prudent approach to decision making minimizes risk while empowering you to make significant changes in your life.

- *Open-ended decisions.* A married couple I know was having a difficult time deciding whether to have children. So they made an open-ended decision instead; simply to stop using birth control and see what happens. As it turned out, they did have a child—and they were delighted. "For us, it had all the authenticity of a real, full-blown decision," the woman notes. "Even when I was pregnant and we began to wonder what we had gotten ourselves into, the knowledge that we had decided, that we were in agreement, let us both feel that we were moving ahead out of a real commitment." In certain situations, deciding to "roll the dice" can be an effective approach that opens the door for change to occur.

- *Limited-control decisions.* At times, we can decide to "control what we can" and act anyway. This is the paradigm at work in military operations when a decision is made to invade or advance against an enemy. The army will be prepared, move ahead, make adjustments along the way, and hopefully prevail.

A similar paradigm exists in sports. A golfer, for example, makes certain decisions about how to play a particular hole. Which club should she use? How should she swing? What should her overall strategy be for the hole? The golfer is making decisions that, tangentially at best, will determine the outcome. Yet without those decisions, she drastically reduces her chances of playing competitively.

Be courageous. This too sounds simple, yet seldom is. There is always some risk in making a decision. The more important and life-altering the decision is, the greater the risk will be. Yet if you are not courageous about decisions, you are committing yourself to a life without change. The dangers of inaction are even greater than the risks of the decision you are contemplating.

In many decisions a moment does arise when you need to say, "There is a risk to this. I understand it. I've minimized the problems that might arise as a result of my decision. I can't make the risk go away completely. I have to accept the risk and act anyway by taking a step, despite the fact that it's worrying me."

You will usually find that, whatever the undertaking, you can rise to its challenges and make it work. "I assumed leadership of a counseling center and I needed to put together a board," a psychotherapist told me recently. "I didn't know how, but I just went ahead anyway. Needless to say, I learned along the way and made it happen."

The courage to act is hastened by a healthy amount of self-confidence and knowledge that you have the flexibility to meet new challenges. Such courage isn't foolhardiness. It's the kind of decisiveness that separates the "doers" from the "nondoers" in the process of life.

My Friends Joanne and Jacques

My friend Joanne spent years in unsuccessful relationships with many different men. When a relationship broke up, her usual explanation was, "He was dull," or "He had no sense of adventure," or "He never read anything interesting."

Then one day she struck up a relationship with Jacques, an accomplished French photojournalist who traveled from one world hot spot to another. He even outgunned Joanne in her reading—he absorbed almost everything in sight. Better yet, he knew some of the authors whose books meant the most to Joanne.

Interestingly enough, Jacques flipped for Joanne and wanted to marry her.

Now Joanne had a decision to make. Was she ready to make a commitment or not? What was she going to do? At last, all the excuses she'd relied on in the past were pulled out from under her.

Develop a healthy skepticism toward authority. Too may people delay making decisions because they haven't taken specific steps or made the requisite preparations for the kinds of actions they are contemplating.

"I have a dynamite idea for an article *The New York Times* might like," says a college senior. "But don't you have to publish articles in a lot of other places before you even go to the *Times* with an idea? Won't they shoot me down?"

In a similar vein, a young actress says, "I just got out of acting school and people say I have a spectacular Broadway singing voice. Don't I need to spend a lot of time in regional theaters before I take the big step and audition for a New

York show? Won't the producers want to see a long résumé before they hire me?"

A Place for Each Decision-Making Style

A company made up entirely of P-style decision makers would probably be a disaster. Decisions would be made impulsively, based on hunches and emotions alone. Running a company requires consideration as well as emotion.

On the flip side, an emergency rescue team would be unable to do its job if it were made up entirely of J-style decision makers. If I were injured and in need of immediate attention, I'd look for people who could decide immediately what needed to be done, and take quick action.

Neither decision-making style is right. But there are circumstances where one, or the other, is demanded.

Well, these two people might be right. They could try to sell their wares in the most important arenas in their chosen professions, or they could choose to wait. But a more important consideration here is: "What's the downside of trying?" A rejection letter from *The New York Times* or an unsuccessful audition wouldn't be the end of their careers, after all. And the upside of simply trying might be tremendous.

Most successful people owe their successes to "breaks" or sudden leaps forward. By developing a healthy disrespect for artificial boundaries and power structures, you increase the chances that those breaks will come your way.

Watch for signs of external confirmation. This may sound like curious advice in a practical, down-to-earth book.

But I firmly believe that when we make sound decisions—sometimes, when we are only contemplating them—the world moves with us in visible ways. We get signs that we are on the right path.

Sometimes, these external signs of confirmation can seem routine, almost obvious.

"I took a job in Chicago and moved my whole family there," an executive says. "Would you believe, our neighbors have two kids about the same ages as our own? My new job is working out great. We even found a church that seems to be an ideal match for our outlook and beliefs. It's kind of like all this was meant to happen."

At other times, confirming signs are more subtle.

The Limiting Power of Decisions

Some life decisions close the path to other decisions. If you decide to take a job in Chicago, you won't be living in New York. If you decide to go to law school, you will probably not become a doctor.

This sounds limiting, but it is really a way of determining the content of your life. You're making choices, deciding what is most important and what is secondary.

It makes me think of Robert Frost's well-known poem "The Road Not Taken." Most people interpret that poem as a symbol of Frost's life: He could have taken a well-traveled road, but chose to become a poet instead. At another level of meaning all of us move through life, making choices at significant crossroads when we find them. Through choices, we travel the road of life that is most authentic for who we are.

"I was trying to decide whether to change my career and go into publishing," a woman recalls, "and I suddenly noticed that I was starting to meet more people who worked in publishing. Maybe I was just more on the watch for them, it's true. But the fact is, I began to develop a new circle of acquaintances who were able to provide me with advice and guidance, right when I needed it."

I firmly believe that when you are about to embark on the right track, signs of confirmation do come from "out there" somewhere. You are being welcomed and buoyed. By heeding these messages, you can gain confirmation—and courage—to make the right decision.

EXERCISES

1. **Create a prioritized inventory of pending decisions.** Over a period of days or weeks, jot down all the decisions you are trying to make in your life. Some may appear quite mundane. Should you repaint your bedroom or install wallpaper? Is it time to buy a new printer for your home office? Should you talk to your son's teacher at school because you are troubled by his attitude at home?

   Other pending decisions may stun you with their overriding importance. Should you tell your spouse you are unfulfilled in certain areas of your relationship—get it out in the open and work on it—or should you keep the problem bottled up? You will find that you have many more pending decisions working than you might have suspected.

As your list grows, try to develop categories for important and less important choices you are faced with making. Also, prioritize the list. Which decisions should you make now? Which ones can wait until later? Make a special "need more info" note beside any decisions for which that is the case.

Armed with your list, you can better understand the decision-making work you need to do to move your life forward.

2. **Understand your decision-making style.** You may want to take the Myers-Briggs test to better understand the way you process information before making up your mind. Alternatively, you can talk to your spouse or friends and ask for their observations about how you approach the decisions in your life.

Do you hesitate, even after you know enough to move ahead? Do you act too impulsively? Do you fail to act because you are afraid? Do you resist change because you are too comfortable? The answers to such questions may send you clear signals that it is time to revise your decision-making style—possibly to take action on decisions you have been postponing.

3. **Analyze decisions you've made in the past.** Look at the really big ones—the decisions about which college to attend, where to move, whom to marry. Catalog the decisions and then consider both how you approached them and what the outcomes were.

Were there times when you waited too long to make a decision, for instance? Or were there times when you erred by making an important decision without the benefit of sufficient research or inquiry into the choice you were facing?

By learning more about your decision-making history, you can learn to make better decisions in the future.

4. **Push the risk envelope.** From the prioritized decision inventory you created in exercise 1, select one decision which you currently feel unprepared to make. Try to move it ahead anyway and see what happens. This exercise might result in a small setback, it's true. But it might also lead you to make more decisions, and make them more courageously, as you decide your way through life.

5 PUT KARMA ON YOUR SIDE

A few weeks ago, some interesting, seemingly chance events befell a business friend of mine named Paul. They were the kinds of "random" occurrences that made him wonder whether anything truly random ever occurs at all.

First, something bad happened to Paul. While parking his van, he scraped the car behind him. Instead of tip-toeing away from the scene, he wrote a note that apologized and included his phone number. He tucked it under the windshield wiper of the car he had damaged. Sure enough, the car's owner called the next day, and Paul went to a body shop and wrote a check for $250 for the repair. The owner of the damaged car was, to say the least, thankful for Paul's honesty.

Then, when Paul got home from the body shop, some remarkable things started to happen. First, the mail brought a check for $750 for a professional fee he had completely forgotten he had coming. Next, the phone rang and it was a new client—someone Paul had been

(Continued on next page.)

(Continued from previous page.)

courting to no avail—who now said he was ready to hire Paul as a consultant.

All that led Paul to recall the words of Jesus: "What you sow you will also reap." Similarly Jewish sages and rabbis have long advised people to perform "mitz-vahs"—positive, selfless acts to benefit others—in the belief that such actions will attract positive benefits in life. In the words popularized by a Willie Nelson song: "What goes around comes around."

Now, Paul knew these beliefs and sayings, but he was incredulous. Were good things really happening to him because he had done a good thing? Or was it all just coincidence?

Well, it wasn't coincidence. It never is. In fact, with the right attitude and practices, you can put the transforming forces of good karmic energy to work for you. Paul did it—without even knowing he was doing so.

Let's find out how to get the power of karma working for you.

References to karma seem to be everywhere in our culture today. The word has been cropping up more and more since the 1960s, when Eastern religion began to exert such a strong influence on popular Western culture. Blame it on the Beatles.

We turn to karma when we need to rationalize inexplicable things out of our control. If we get into a fender bender, for example, we conveniently proclaim, "Not my fault! Just bad karma." Or if another candidate gets the job we just interviewed for, we shrug it off with, "Well, it wasn't my day. Just my karma." On the other hand, if we narrowly miss hitting that other car or we do get that job offer we wanted, we chalk it up to "good karma" and happily collect its rewards. Then we don't give it another thought.

So it seems that karma gives us stuff. Or karma takes it away. *Karma is just like that. It's all out of our hands.*

This is the popular view of karma. It lets us conveniently, quickly recycle any experience. Whatever happens, we cannot be blamed. We are passive bystanders who live out the words of that Willie Nelson song, or the sentiment on that bumper sticker "Stuff Happens."

Such popular concepts—which portray karma as a sort of out-of-control, cosmic gorilla—have no basis in Hinduism or Buddhism, the two religions that most closely monitor karma's curious workings. In fact, the purest, original law of karma presents a view that is the opposite of the popular, passive one that has taken hold in our culture. Karma is actually a Sanscrit word that means action or work. *Passive acceptance has nothing to do with it. Taking action is the key.*

The real law of karma is that the things that come to us in life are the direct results of the actions we have taken. That's what my friend Paul glimpsed, and that's what can happen for you.

KARMA IS RESPONSIBILITY

What a revelation! We are not passive pawns in life, waiting for good or bad karma to land on us. We control everything! We're in charge! We make things shake with every action we take. We can toss pebbles into our karmic pool and wait for good things to come back to us. We don't have to wait passively. We can actually start good things moving in our direction.

Yet we must also be aware of the negative side of the equation—a cosmic exhortation to behave and act well.

The Cosmic Boomerang

If you take the right actions in life (performing what is called a mitzvah in Hebrew: doing good in any form), karma will reward you with a good life. If you perform negative acts, bad things will happen to you.

Remember, karma means action. Each little step we take in life sets up a dynamic buzz in the universe—a cosmic vibration that comes back to us. It's like a cosmic boomerang that keeps reappearing in day-to-day life. There's no escaping it!

"All our experiences will be thrust on us, whether we want them or not," writes one Hindu sage. That's a sobering thought! But it is also an empowering one, telling us we have the ability to bring about wonderful things in our lives by taking positive actions, rather than negative ones.

I also like this explanation of karma, which appeared in a recent article in *Hinduism Today:* "Each karma, or action, generates a vibration, a distinct oscillation of force . . . acts of love attract loving acts, malice attracts malice."

The Butterfly Effect Revisited

The scientific principle known as the butterfly effect offers another way to look at karma. According to the theory, if a butterfly in China moves its wings, the weather all around the world will be affected—even as far away as North America.

The result may not be perceptible or quantifiable in scientific terms. Still, the change really is there. Similarly, the many small actions we take in the world have an effect. And the more little good actions we take, the more good things will come back to us.

Here's a story that illustrates the positive results that can result from good actions.

A woman I know named Paula inherited a "mess" when she became coach of her daughter's soccer team. The last coach left the team in complete disarray—a ragtag group of nice kids who lost most games. There was no money in the budget for new uniforms, travel, or equipment. Parents were grumpy and uncooperative. They felt bruised from their encounters with the former coach, who was negative and abrasive. Worst of all, the team members themselves were burned out, tired of the game.

Predictably, Paula's first practice was a frustrating disaster. But then, things changed. While driving home, she happened to pass a park. Although she was discouraged, she noticed that the park was full of litter. It badly needed a cleaning up. Because she felt the need to do something positive to break her team's cycle of negativity, Paula decided to hold the team's next practice in that park the following Saturday. Before working on soccer skills, the players would clean up the park. It was a simple attempt to build team spirit, but her idea got the cold-shoulder treatment from parents, who thought the team should be working on passing and running drills.

But the team showed up anyway. Soon, the park was swarming with two dozen kids, each armed with a garbage bag. Paula had not noticed before, but there was a car dealer located across the street from the park. Its owner came out to ask who they were and what they were doing. Within five minutes, he offered to buy new jerseys and equipment for the team. He went back to his showroom and called the editor of the local newspaper, who sent out a photographer on the spot.

My father often helped other people. Yet if we asked him about it, he'd reply that he did it "just in case I ever need anything . . . ."

Was this his own form of karma—or perhaps a simple application of the Golden Rule?

By the time the kids left the park, they were feeling pretty positive about the day. Getting your picture in the paper has that effect! The parents were feeling more upbeat too. Other good things continued to happen. The car dealer got several businesses to support the team. Now, it would be an exaggeration to say Paula's team went on to win the state championships. That would happen in a Hollywood screenplay, not necessarily in real life. But as it turned out, she was able to provide her daughter's team with a very positive experience for the year.

So we see that one positive act attracts like acts. That's the power of karma in action. When you're stuck, doing one positive thing is sometimes all that is required to break the logjam and start positive things coming your way. It's truly a miracle that can work for you.

THE KARMIC TIME FRAME

When will your karmic payback come? If you put a penny in the panhandler's cup as you walk down Main Street, will you find a dollar when you turn the corner onto Elm? If you send your soccer team to tidy up the park, will a friendly car dealer always appear and offer to buy you jerseys?

Maybe yes, maybe no. Some good acts seem to produce an immediate payback from "out there" somewhere. Others produce little. Or perhaps they pay you back much later, in ways you do not expect or recognize. You send an aging uncle a check to cover his medical expenses and then, five years later, you unexpectedly receive a plane ticket to Paris from his grateful son. It sounds farfetched, but such things do happen. And if they do, do they represent actual karmic payback for the things you have done?

Newtonian Karma

The workings of karma resemble one of Newton's physical laws: "For every action there is an equal and opposite reaction." Or, in popular culture, "What goes around comes around."

But the bottom line with karma is that every action attracts a parallel reaction—good for good, bad for bad. Either you can fight this powerful flow or you can swim with it.

Maybe yes. Maybe no. To reap positive karmic rewards, you have to set aside cause-and-effect considerations. You have to just keep doing good.

I'm reminded of the Bible parable of casting loaves of bread on the water. Some loaves come back, others may not. You cannot expect a fresh new loaf for each one that floats away. You've got to keep on doing good, without expectation of payback.

As Carl Jung observed, the links between cause and effect may never become clear to us in what we do. We need to have faith in the overall process—casting loaves, doing good: simply taking a positive role in life.

Karma works. Perhaps it's the butterfly effect. Perhaps it's that cosmic backwash, reestablishing order in the world. Whatever it is, it works when we choose positive action as our way of connecting with people and with the world.

Immediate Payback

Sometimes karma operates in quite a tight time frame.

I have a friend who, while a student, was a paid member of a church choir. One week he got irritated with the organist and skipped choir rehearsal. He was normally a reliable young man, but he did not even bother to call the choir director to say he would not be there.

Instead of attending the rehearsal, he went to the movies with a friend. Midway through the movie, a woman who was sitting in front of him jumped up, pointed an accusing finger in his face, and yelled, "If you don't stop that, I'll call the manager!" She stomped off and sat in a vacant seat. People eyed my friend uneasily. (He swears he was not doing anything but watching the film.)

So there is an example—a pretty amusing one, actually—of immediate karmic payback for a negative act. It's a story my friend loves to tell. Yet the outcome seems troubling on some level. My friend believes that the yelling woman embodied karmic payback for his irresponsible actions. But was that true, or was it just coincidence or "perceived karmic response"—a sequence of events that appeared connected, but actually were not?

Negative Karma

While I was on the highway the other day, another driver cut me off. Just as I was about to honk or try to cut him off in turn, I saw that he had dents and scrapes all over his rather new car. His negative karmic energy was very graphically displayed. I decided to say and do nothing. Good choice! I didn't want to get mixed up in his negative energy field.

It would be nice to figure out such questions—to understand where we stand in the ebb and flow of good acts and bad. Of course, we cannot. We simply go through life doing what we do, and different things happen to us. How do we know what is in response to what?

Clearly, punishment for bad actions doesn't fall upon everyone. We've all known people who have gone through life mistreating others, with few apparent negative consequences. Yet who knows how those people feel, or how well or badly life rewards them?

Life-to-Life Payback

Hinduism grants karma a lot of time to establish equilibrium. Because if we don't get things right in our current lifetime, we have many more lives to come! In fact, Hindu sages have identified at least four separate kinds of karma.

- *Kriyayama karma.* This is the karma contained in the daily actions we take. By taking an action—good or bad—we both release this karmic energy into the world and accumulate some of it, as the following form of karma called Sanchita.

- *Sanchita karma.* This is the body of karma that each of us stores up during our lifetimes. As we live and take action, we are contributing to this personal karmic pool.

- *Prarabdha karma.* This is the body of karma that we bring with us into the world, accumulated in our previous lifetimes. It predates and causes our births.

- *Agami karma.* This is the karma that comes back to us from the world—the eventual result of actions we have taken in the world and the karma we accumulated in previous lifetimes. It is the payback, for better or worse, for what we have done in this lifetime and previous ones.

Eastern religious texts, in fact, have defined many other gradations of karma. There is the karma that is accumulated and shared by nations, families, even races. You might be living with bad karma because of some negative actions your father took!

So, what about this "other" karma—the kind that is carried on from one lifetime to the next? What about the karma that's stored up for you, from before you were born?

From my side of the equation, as a Western man rooted in the Judeo-Christian religions, I have to admit that I have trouble with the notion of reincarnation. I have a hard time accepting the idea that, if we don't get around to working out our root issues in this lifetime, we still have time. We're evolving from a less enlightened being to a more enlightened one as we move from life to life.

I'm not dismissing the possibility of reincarnation. In fact, I have Christian and Jewish friends who do not find the idea to be at odds with their own religious beliefs. Yet somehow, for me, the most potent karmas to put into use are the Kriyayama and Agami varieties—the karmas that we accumulate daily and that come back to us in our lifetimes. In other words, I prefer to think in terms of the actions I am taking and the kinds of results they bring to me.

This should be enough reincarnation to think about:

"The sins of the father are visited on the children."

So for the purposes of this book, let's focus on what we can do in our own lives—actions that will impact on us personally. (If you are comfortable with the idea that your karma may be accumulated and lived out from one lifetime to the next, I encourage you to explore Hinduism more fully by reviewing the recommended readings at the end of the book.)

Putting Karma to Work for You

Now that you have glimpsed the outline of karma's workings, how can you begin to experiment with it? To put it into play in your life? How, let's say, can you take karma for a test drive?

Like Paula the soccer coach, you can get the karmic "ball rolling" by performing some experimental, positive acts. Yet, truth to tell, just doing good may not be the answer.

The karmic sages tell us that just doing good may not lead to a happier life. To increase the positive returns we may get from doing good, we have to understand distinct stages of karmic activity and engage in them consciously.

Cultivate a desire to do good. You can't perform actions that are generous or kind just because you expect something in return. You must first cultivate a real desire to do good—a pure heart, in a manner of speaking.

Perform the good deeds themselves. It's not enough to have good intentions. You also need to actively do good in the real world. The process of doing good begins *in your hearts* and moves *out into the real world.*

Accept frustrations and irritations, and keep going anyway. The karmic scholars are very clear on this! Pursuing a path of good works is paved with frustrations, lean periods, and misunderstandings. Yet you must keep going and remain committed to doing good, even when no payback arrives.

Now that you have glimpsed the outline of karma's workings, how can you begin to experiment with it? To put it into play in your life?

The Three Steps to Getting Your Karma Jump-Started

First, Cultivate a Desire to do Good

I know a successful entrepreneur who is chairman of the board of a cultural foundation, apparently with the sole intention of winning influence and softening his reputation as a cutthroat businessman. He is continually frustrated when the money he spends on this foundation fails to win him real respect or acceptance by members of the cultural and social circles he aspires to. He's left on the sidelines and he's getting angry!

Could it be that this man lacks the pure heart and commitment that would let him attain the results he desires? Or, is it that he acts in expectation of a good return for his actions, so he gets no satisfaction? In other words, he lacks a selfless desire to do good.

Second, Perform the Good Deeds Themselves

I'm reminded of the joke about a rich man who dies. As in all such jokes, he is quizzed at heaven's gates by St. Peter, who asks, "Why do you deserve entry into heaven?"

The rich man replies, "I clothed the poor, fed my poor neighbors, and tended to the sick."

(Continued on next page.)

(Continued from previous page.)

When St. Peter inquires, "Did you really?" the man answers, "Well, no, but I meant to." So the message is, intention is not enough. Your plans for good deeds need to be put into action.

Third, Accept Frustrations and Irritations, and Keep Going Anyway

An acquaintance of mine, after flirting with "other women" for years, finally resolved to mend his ways and devote his affections solely to his wife. It was not an easy commitment for him to make or adhere to, since he apparently judged his masculinity and effectiveness in life on his sexual allure. But he realized in his heart that if he didn't change, he was going to lose someone he really loved.

When he had committed to change, the man told his wife about his decision. She rebuffed him strongly. She had heard it all before. (In fact, she had!) Now, her husband was being truthful instead of lying—a development she had no way of knowing about.

The man had to invest several years in acting on his new commitment before his wife sensed that he had really changed. And it took even longer before she trusted him!

A JUDEO-CHRISTIAN PERSPECTIVE ON LIVING A KARMIC LIFE

As we take these steps to invite karma into our lives, can't we also ask, "Does what I am doing further the kingdom of heaven? And what about my evolutionary life?" In other words, can we bring a Judeo-Christian perspective to doing good in the world?

> Desiring to do good and even doing good are not, in themselves, enough to attain karmic rewards. You have to be willing to hang with the process for the long haul. Doing good has to become a part of your character and be present at all times, even when no one thanks you. This is one time when virtue may truly be its own reward!

One of my favorite New Testament parables is that of the sower. As Jesus describes the kingdom of heaven, he says, "The kingdom of God is like the sower of seeds. The sower goes forth and scatters seeds back and forth across the field." So in the parable, seeds are falling on both fertile ground and infertile, on rocks as well as soil.

Now, when I was a kid growing up in the Midwest and I first heard this parable, I thought, "Boy, that's a dumb way to sow seeds! I know about farming and a farmer is supposed to plow the field and make neat, little rows and then put the seeds in. And soon, there will be nice, neat rows of crops."

In biblical days, of course, farmers first scattered seeds all over the field, then plowed them into the earth. The seeds that fell on good soil would grow into plants, the others that landed in the brambles or on rocks wouldn't. Jesus' point was that some of the good actions we take will be effective; others will wither and die on the rocks. Which does which is beyond our control. His imagery gives a wonderful model for the way karma works. We sow good deeds without regard to payback.

To reap life's rewards, we must become selfless sowers of worthy acts, even if the world doesn't recognize or thank us. That's what the sages of Eastern religion mean when they talk about living a "skillful" life. I like to call it an effective life.

Like Meets Like

People who are unable to establish lasting relationships often complain, "I seem to attract the same kind of people into my life—the wrong kind. Why do I attract them over and over again?"

A woman who is working on issues of availability, for example, often attracts men who are unavailable—men who are working through the same issue themselves. Or a man who can't establish intimacy attracts women who have the same inabilities and blocks.

I doubt these people are working out negative karma from prior lives, but I do suspect that most of them are living with results of their own life actions.

After all, we not only attract events and fortune to ourselves, but we attract people as well. The energies that we send out bring resonant people into our lives.

Whatever the right word for this kind of life is, it is active, positive, selfless, and giving.

We have all known people who have lived that kind of life, and I think that we have witnessed the kinds of rewards that have accrued to them and to the people who shared their lives.

Living that kind of life is a decision you can make. I'd urge you to make that decision now.

Performing Esteemable Acts

I learned about "esteemable acts" from an unlikely source— a recovering alcoholic who attended Alcoholics Anonymous meetings. Even though he had stopped drinking years ago, he was still working on issues related to his "alcoholic personality." For him, giving up drinking was easier than what followed.

Recalling his drinking years, he said, "I was lying, cheating, stealing. No one could count on me for anything. Everything I did was a lie. Everything I promised, I could never deliver. I could never say, 'I'll be there,' because I could never know whether I'd be there or not."

He hated living like that. He hated seeing himself reflected that way in other people's eyes. And a major part of his own recovery became doing what AA terms "esteemable acts." In effect, he accepted that the actions he performed would literally determine who he would become. So he changed all his stuff around. He worked on being very honest. He worked on being on time. He worked on keeping his promises. He worked on venerating the people he loved—on treating them well, being reliable, not cheating on them.

He worked hard on not telling one person one thing and another person another thing. He started to sift his whole life through a new grid, looking at it in a new way. In his way, he was working on attaining the kind of skillful life that is the cornerstone of karmic religion. It was not an easy path, but in the end, it empowered him to heal both his own life and the lives of the people around him.

So we see that actions hurt, but that actions can also heal.

Roadblocks in the Path

Assuming that you are able to conceive of good works and then do them, how can you fail to benefit from engaging in the karmic process? Essentially, you can't. Yet we also know that it is possible to do good things and never see the benefits—either to ourselves or to others.

What's going on when this happens? What's blocking the karmic flow? Let's turn again to the writings of the karmic sages, who have identified the roadblocks that can cut off the benefits of karmic give and take.

Cravings. In our materialistic world, most of us actively desire a number of things that we don't really need. Sometimes, we even crave things that we don't actually want. And those cravings can impede the path of pure karmic action taking.

A friend told me about a bumper sticker that says, "Want What You Have!" Apparently, it was distributed by an organization fighting materialistic attitudes. Whatever its source, I think it offers one approach to thinking about desires in a more enlightened way.

Cravings

Some years back, I spent some time talking with a successful stock broker. After receiving a large bonus one year, he went right out and bought a $100,000 Porsche. When he drove up in his driveway and realized that he had spent nearly his entire bonus on it, he sensed that the car represented an empty victory.

He told me, "I don't even like cars that much. I'm driving this thing, it cost $100,000, I can't park it anywhere. Everybody thinks I'm getting snooty. I spent my whole bonus, which I could have spent on a lot of things that would be much more rewarding to me."

He learned a very difficult lesson—one that many of us have probably learned in our lives. Sometimes, when we want something very badly and then get it, it's a big letdown.

There are cravings of a nonmaterial nature too—and they can also interfere with good karma. That's the case, I think, with a woman I know who studies painting because she wants to impress people with a nice, big still-life over her couch. Now, if she were truely interested in painting, she might someday create images that brought joy to people. But because she is not really learning to paint, that will never happen. She is using paint and brushes to play some other game that lies outside of the process she thinks she is engaged in! Because she has gotten mired in ill-defined cravings and expectations, she has short-circuited her own karmic cycle and gotten stuck.

Such cravings can interfere with our ability to do good for others. They prevent us from making the best use of our resources, send our lives down frustrating dead-ends, and cut us off from the kinds of rewards that karma provides for good, selfless activities.

Resistance. Resistance is a block that people put between themselves and their true desires. Many people, it seems, resist life itself. They innoculate themselves against life by creating a concept of where their lives are supposed to go. Then, when reality does not match up, they can't regroup and go with the change.

Curiously, resistance doesn't occur only when we're unsuccessful or blocked by obvious obstacles. In fact, we often resist hardest when things are going quite well for us. We resist because our egos blind us to the good things that karma is bringing. They just don't fit into our script. To benefit from karma, we've got to get out of the way and simply receive what life is bringing.

What's happening with you? Pretty good, isn't it? If life doesn't match your plan, maybe it's time to respect this "other" agenda and get in flow with hidden processes. Karma may be trying to tell you something, shouting to be heard over the din of your ego and plans.

Resistance

A childhood friend grew up with familial expectations that he would be a successful businessman. That's the yardstick he used when taking stock of his accomplishments and success.

Now, he is also a model father and husband, blessed with a wonderful and loving family—factors he viewed as "extras" in the overall scheme of his life. Mostly, he worked. His appearance at the family dinner table was rare, usually only on weekends. He traveled a lot.

When he lost his corporate job and was unemployed for a period of time, he felt he had failed his family terribly. When he took on a new job as a real estate salesman (the only job he was able to find, and a "stopgap" until he could get back on the executive track), he felt even more remorseful because he was not going to earn as much as he had before. When the lease on his Mercedes expired, he rented a "ho-hum" car instead and felt bad each time he saw his wife drive away in it.

My friend was resisting change stubbornly, just digging in his heels. Only a year later did he realize that his new work status was not harming his loved ones, it was helping them. What they needed from him most was not his money, but his presence and his love. As his wife explained, "We were elated to have him back in our lives. He was finally elated to be back too, but it took him some time to realize that his career change was a blessing, not a curse."

A blessing in disguise!

Delusions. We all have them! Some people believe their judgment is infallible. Others think that there is some higher power that will inevitably intervene to save them when life's disasters loom. We all have such illusions and delusions. We see them half-hidden behind the belief systems that we use to make decisions and operate in the world.

Delusions

Carl Jung, the Swiss psychologist, believed that there was a force or "plan" for our lives and that we should not fight it, but get in line with it. Otherwise life would run over us like a steamroller.

The result of our resistance will be frustration—even mental illness and a kind of psychic death. How much better to get in line with the process!

Yet the real question is: Which delusions do *you* have? To confound you in the search for the answer to that question, there is one additional problem: The delusions that limit you the most are probably those that are most invisible to you.

So we see that karma is something we can engage in actively, but cannot control or command. That seems like a contradiction to most of us Westerners, but if you can hold the two possibilities of control and lack of control in tension, an interesting relationship to karma can result.

I knew an investment banker who was faced with the decision of making time for his job or making time to find a woman to share his life with. He consistently decided that the job came first. I finally said to him, "You know, the deals you're doing are important, I don't want to minimize them. But you could win all the battles of your life and lose the war. There's a lot of 'larger context' stuff that's not being served here." The man had achieved great financial success, but he was on a dead-end track in his life.

As we discussed and explored his situation, we uncovered a kind of central delusion that colored his life and directed his decisions along the wrong path. We discovered that he thought he was going to live forever! There was no time line in his life, no need to find a partner, no hurry to make the big decisions. He had plenty of time. "When I get older, I'll worry about having that relationship," he thought.

This man's thought pattern was faulty, out of touch with reality. Yet doesn't his attitude offer a glimpse at our own lives—how delusions seduce us into thinking that we are in control, when we are not? In his case, delusions had led him to a state of denial and, ultimately, to the creation of a life that was not authentic for him.

THREE KEYS TO GETTING ATTUNED TO YOUR KARMA

As I close this chapter, let me set out a four-part process for getting your karmic ball rolling.

Step 1: Learn from life. Learn from what life gives you. Take every event that happens to you, whether good or bad. Accept it and learn from it. Not every event in our lives yields up its meaning to inspection. Not every event has profound content. But keeping attuned to what life brings up deepens our experience and opens the karmic process to new levels.

Learn from Life

Not long ago, a friend of mine was waiting for a train when he was approached by a traveler who needed help setting the time on his digital watch. Soon, three or four people were trying to get this young man's watch set correctly.

It was an insignificant encounter in many ways—one that most of us would forget in the course of a day or two. Yet my friend felt that there were threads of meaning woven into the encounter—messages about his own reactions to other people, messages about time and its meaning, messages about human kindness and expectations.

No doubt, you too have had experiences in which people suddenly appeared in your life, bringing unexpected messages. Don't judge those people or dismiss them or categorize them. Instead, accept them as messengers who bear some kind of higher information and utilize them as a chance to learn something about life and about yourself.

Consider, too, every person in your life—your friends, colleagues, spouse or life partner. Karma has placed them in your life for definite reasons—albeit complex. Understanding why those people are in your life is an ongoing process that teaches you about both karma's workings and about yourself.

This is especially true with our closest friends and loved ones. If we have woven deep life tapestries with these people, they are involved with our karma on the most profound levels. They have much to teach us!

Step 2: Increase your esteemable acts. As you act and live your life from day to day, ask, "Am I doing what I want for my life, as the kind of person I want to be? Am I saying the things I want to say? Am I spending my time on the right things? Do I make the right decisions? Is each decision I make best for me and for my world?" Strive to put everything you do through this grid of esteemable acts and stay in touch with the kind of person you would really like to be.

Learn from People

Think about the people in your life. You don't have chance relationships. People are sent to you.

You can learn a lot if you ask, "Why is this person in my life right now?" or " Why do I enjoy the company of this kind of person?"

Ask these questions. Learn. Be a student of life.

Step 3: Take leadership for your life. Don't think of leadership as something that is practiced by CEOs or politicians. We each can assume a leadership role in our own lives, if we can claim it. Claim that role and do not let it pass you by.

Step 4: Be patient in the face of adversity. As a therapist and clergyman, I am often faced with the difficult task of listening to people who seem to be stuck in their problems. I would love to find a way to snap people instantly out! Yet that would deprive them of the opportunity to grow and learn from the process they are engaged in.

Each of us, after all, needs to be patient in our suffering— to struggle with the issues that trouble us, to pray about them, and to allow time to work out our own salvation. We need our suffering, in a sense, because it is one of the means to becoming the kind of people we want to be. The struggle is always worth it because it moves us along the karmic road.

But the promise of karma is that being patient with the struggles of our lives—while we continue to act—will eventually lead to wonderful things.

Take Leadership for Your Life

My friend Edith was often frustrated in her relationship with her husband. "I'm sick of him," she told me. "He feels like an immovable weight. I can't get him to do anything. He's a couch potato and he's getting worse. The older he gets, the more he sits on the couch. He comes home from work, flops down, and turns on the TV. I can't get him to do anything."

I asked, "What would you like him to do?"

She said, "Oh, I don't know. I'm too tired to know anymore. I'm too tired to fight to make us get out and do anything. I always have to do it. I'm always the one."

I tried to help Edith take action—for herself, at least, because she had given even that up. I urged her, "Sometimes your husband will be the leader, doing what he wants. But you need to take that role too. Don't cooperate yourself into a corner."

Finally, she did take action. Instead of remaining paralyzed, she started to walk, exercise, and get back into the world. When her husband saw that this was the direction her life was taking, he started to join in. But the first step was for Edith to do what she needed to do, for *herself*.

You have to take leadership for your own life. If you remain stuck, waiting for another person to act, you can never take action. Do something. That's the surest way to break negative behavior patterns—yours or someone else's.

EXERCISES

1. **Identify and overcome cravings.** Spend a few minutes thinking about cravings you may have—as well as addictions or obsessions. Talk with a good friend, your spouse, or a confidant such as a minister or rabbi. List possible cravings on a piece of paper and, under each, outline the possible negative outcomes you may be living with. Then make a vow to yourself to strive to give up each negative block to good karma.

   Example: "Hoarding money keeps me from freely spending what I need to enjoy my life. It keeps me from being generous with my friends. Vow: I will save only the portion of my income necessary to establish a reasonable cushion of safety and to fund an adequate retirement program. I will invest the rest in my life and in living life to the fullest."

2. **Overcome resistance points.** Sit a while and meditate on the resistance points in your life. What are you afraid of? In what kinds of situations do you "hit the brakes" or drag your feet? List these tendencies and write down the consequences that each one brings to you. Then make a promise to yourself to try to let go of your resistance points. Follow up with a list of the means you will use to get the job done.

   Example: "I seem to be afraid of flying. It causes me to miss out on seeing interesting places in the world, on having adventures, and on visiting friends and family members. I am going to get over this fear by seeking some behavioral therapy and planning some increasingly distant trips in the future."

3. **Uncover and overcome delusions.** Since delusions are often unconscious, enlist the help of a loved one or trusted friend to discover yours. Ask this person to help you perform a "delusion inventory"—a kind of mental health inventory. Here are some questions to ask:

— Has your confidant noticed ways in which you may be out of touch with reality?

— Do you sometimes behave in ways that don't jibe with the rest of your life?

— Can your friend pinpoint beliefs you hold about yourself or the world that make you miss the mark of your personal reality?

Then talk with your confidant about how you can make changes to rid yourself of limiting delusions and beliefs.

Example: "My confidant told me that I put myself down a lot, make little jokes on myself, and don't take myself seriously sometimes. She pointed out that at a party, I told someone that I can't write very well, which is not true. I've done some fine writing in the past. Why do I do that? What am I going to do to shake those self-limiting delusions and move ahead with my life? I decided to pay more attention to what I say to other people, especially to strangers in social settings, and to stop saying things that put myself down. I realized when I said I wasn't a good writer and other such self-denigrating things, I was making a joke at my own expense. Other people don't really find that appealing or funny."

4. Make an inventory of action-taking tools. Where and how can you begin the process of taking positive karmic actions? As you seek opportunities to do good things in your life, don't overlook the opportunities your life already affords.

— *Treat your family as your greatest resource.* Of course, your family itself offers one of the most important arenas for living esteemably. But don't overlook other opportunities your family affords for performing good karmic acts. You can, for example, work on behalf of your children's schools and activities or get involved with your spouse's activities and concerns.

— *Contribute good acts to your community.* Involvement at any level allows you to contribute to your karmic "pool." From serving on community projects to running for public office, many opportunities exist that invite you in.

— *Get involved in charities and organizations that "speak" to you.* When you get involved in activities and causes that interest you, you find natural outlets for positive actions.

— *Use your place of business as a forum for excellent acts.* Working honorably and well with other people can make an immense contribution to your karma.

— *Forge a deeper spiritual connection with your church, synagogue, or other spiritual community.* Seek out the one setting where your beliefs and actions truly coincide—a place where good actions can really contribute to others' well-being and spiritual growth.

— *Treat your friends and social life as a karmic resource, not just a pastime.* There is no better place than "home" to demonstrate kindness and personal concern for others.

5. **Start keeping a karmic journal.** Using a standard appointment book or ring binder, start keeping track of notably positive events in your life. First, note the dates of any good actions you take on behalf of other people. Second, track the dates of notably good things that happen to you—with special attention to *unexpected* good events.

In time, you may get a clearer picture of the karmic ebb and flow that is at work in your life. Be aware, though, that the point of this exercise is not to attach any quid pro quos to your karmic activity. (To be able to say, for example, "I made a charitable contribution on February 1 and got a new job offer on February 9. It was karma!") The goal is to heighten your awareness of good karmic action in your life. With more awareness, you become better attuned to karma at work—and more alert and aware in your karmic activities.

6 WIELD YOUR WILL

Jack was on top of his game. He was an executive vice president of his company, had a beautiful wife and kids, and was generally well thought of by friends and colleagues alike. At 40 years of age he had the world by the tail, and was shaking it in his direction.

The only trouble was that a congenital heart defect, present in his family for generations, had other plans for him. One day out on the golf course, Jack had a massive heart attack. Luckily, because of quick action on the part of his golf partners, he was spared major damage. But the events of that day left him changed for good.

Afterward he said, "Until that moment I actually thought I was in charge of my life. Whatever I wanted I went after and got. Now I know it is not that simple, and that other forces are at work—forces that lie beyond our own desires, volitions, and plans."

When I was a child growing up in a Christian church in the Midwest, it seemed that one fundamental concept was always being drummed into my head: *Our wills are evil*. We were supposed to look for God's will in our lives, not live according to our own desires and wishes. I guess our ideas of what we wanted for our lives were supposed to be flawed. God knew better than we did what was good for us.

If we were willful, we were trying to get our way. We were living selfishly, only for our own good. It seemed that wanting anything was suspect. If I wanted to be best in my class, I was manifesting my desire to show up others and look good. Wanting things and possessions made me vain or even a crass materialist—and we all know where *that* can lead.

There was an almost total mistrust of the human psyche. Anything a person wanted was regarded with suspicion— just because a human being thought of it! We were supposed to align our wishes and desires with God's will, not our own. To make things worse, I had no idea what was meant by God's will, let alone how I could figure it out. I don't think any of my friends had an idea either, but we all seemed to think that this higher, "other" will was much better than our own.

As I got older, I thought this roundabout way of showing that we were wrong in wanting anything and everything was an elaborate trick, devised by adults, to avoid responsibility. At the same time, I sensed a curious loophole in the system. How could anyone blame me for doing something I thought was God's will? If I could claim that was the case, I could want things. I had nothing to do with it.

Take Your Castor Oil—It's Good For You!

As children, we allowed ourselves to be told what was good for us and what was not. Other people called the shots.

In adulthood, we finally got to make decisions. Yet just when our freedom seemed to be in hand, new issues and questions intruded.

What really is good for us? What is bad? What should we want?

Defining our wants and desires is, all at once, an exercise in freedom and a discovery of new limitations in what we are free to do in our lives.

I also used to think that the complaint about selfishness—that by wanting something, I was being self-indulgent—was a thinly veiled way for parents to control children. In fact, I still do today.

WANTING PUTS OUR LIVES IN MOTION

It is true that our wants lead us around. What we want from our deepest selves determines our direction and vision for our lives. Over time, our inner vision becomes outer reality. Idle wishing doesn't do much, but *wanting* seems to be another matter. When we actively begin to want something, we start planning and putting things in motion.

Far from just being willful for their own sake, our wants and desires point to some of the deepest trends of our inner lives and make them take on a form we can touch and see. In fact, despite all the teachings I heard when I was child, I would not want to live one minute of my life cut off from my will if I could help it.

Far from denigrating the will, I believe we should encourage it and develop it further. I believe that otherwise we will be alienated from the will, which can serve as an inner guide that has much to tell us.

I once worked with a woman who had what she described as "no life syndrome." She reported to me that her life seemed to be directed almost entirely from the external world around her. In fact, she had cultivated the habit of getting herself into situations that were highly structured so that she could always know just what was expected of her.

The lessons she had heard during her childhood were similar to those I had heard; she had learned them well. Great security and even a sense of self would come from doing what others expected and wanted, not following her own path. Her parents raised her that way, and she fell right into step when she moved out of their home to make her own way in the world. It took many years and much encouragement to get her to trust her inner instinctual desires. Finally, she realized that she could free herself and live the kind of life she wanted, for herself. Getting in touch with her wants—her highly personal needs, not those of others—was the key.

HOW MUCH CONTROL DO WE REALLY HAVE?

Is it right for us to be suspicious of people who tell us just to "take charge of our lives," as if we can quickly make up a plan for our lives, and live it out? Set goals and then meet them. Plan your life and then work the plan!

Perhaps you have known people who have tried such approaches. Maybe you have tried them a time or two yourself.

Even though the title of this book is *Take Control of Your Life,* by now you have some idea of the type of control I am talking about. It is a control that matches up our inner wishes with the possibilities around us. It is a harmonious working together of the will and fate—a balance of "what I want" and "what is possible."

Children Wield Their Will

Early in their lives, children are usually in touch with their wants. I watched a young boy in the store the other day. Every aisle he passed through offered him things he desperately wanted.

"I want one of those!" he would cry.

"I want some candy!"

"Mommy, buy that for me!"

I sympathized with the mother, who patiently tried to explain why the boy could not have each item. Finally, in exasperation she sounded a note of reality: "You can't have everything you see."

The child had the last word, and his words answered everything: "But I want it!"

To me, achieving that balance is the very definition of maturity. It is an acceptance of life and its limits, without giving up the dream of the inner self.

When a person's inner dream dies, in a sense that person dies as well. But it is also true that people who live in a fantasy world, ignoring the demands of reality, never really live. They have trouble getting "traction" to move their lives ahead, trouble making dreams into realities, and problems turning wishes into wants, and wants into actions.

We have all known people who are full of ideas and unrealized fantasies about what might have been or could have been.

I knew a man like that once. He had a lot of big ideas which he liberally spread among his friends about the deals he was going to do, the houses he was looking at. At the center of the whole drama, he placed himself as the hero. His tales were obviously set up so he could make himself feel important. Yet those of us who knew this man well knew that he would never do any of the things he talked about. After a while, most of us stopped listening and, in our eyes, this man became more and more of a pathetic figure.

Saddest of all, he was actually a rather intelligent and talented person. With just a little time and effort, he could have done many of the things he bragged about. But he evidently didn't want to go through the struggle and put up with the possibility of hard work and inevitable failures along the way.

WHY SHOULD YOU ACCEPT WILL IN YOUR LIFE?

There is much more to wanting and willing than simple selfishness or a desire for material things. By accepting your wants and desires, you will find you can move your life ahead in some very positive ways that lead you toward a fuller realization of who you really are in the world and what you want to accomplish.

Some of the benefits of a willful life include:

- The satisfaction of seeing your innermost desires and needs become real in your life.

- More success in your life and work—and all areas where you want to accomplish something important or "make your mark."

There are other benefits too, such as an improved ability to provide people around you with what they want and need in the world—not only material things, but their own hearts' desires. If you have children, for instance, they can learn important life lessons from a parent who not only has lofty dreams and visions, but also has the will to make them become real in life.

HOW TO GET WILL WORKING FOR YOU

Now that we have unmasked will and found it to be beneficial in our lives, rather than destructive, how can we get it working for us? Here are a few approaches:

Get over your negative ideas about wanting something. If you get guilty feelings every time you ask for something or want something, examine where these beliefs came from and be honest with yourself about whether you really feel that way.

Consider your personal past and "script." If your parents taught you to be humble and not ask for anything—to wait for opportunities to be handed to you—they may have programmed you in such a way that knowing your inner desires is going to be difficult. If you agree with ideas like that and

Two Families, Two Daughters

I went to elementary school with two girls, Doreen and Susan. They were the best of friends.

Doreen's parents had their own business, and the family seemed quite successful. Doreen graduated nearly first in her high school class. She attended a top college. I expect she is doing well in her life.

Susan's father tried several business ventures, didn't do well, and finally resigned himself to working as a salesman. He seemed unhappy. Susan's mother stayed home and was known to have a problem with alcohol. Susan was an average student, and the one girl in her class who became pregnant while in high school.

I believe that parents who live willfully, who have ambitions and act on them, give their children a vital set of skills to forge better lives—the ability to act on their dreams.

honestly mistrust your own desires, there may be some deeper-seated negative attitudes about yourself that you should explore.

Not asking for too much, it seems, can be a particular problem for women. Here's how one woman I know explains it:

"I was taught not to ask for too much, and not to expect too much. In our family system, helping others to get what they needed was of paramount importance for all women. Now, helping others get what they need might be important if you're going to be a parent, or if you have to care for an ailing parent for a time. But making it the center of your life doesn't help you get a dynamic life for yourself."

Exercise

Think back over the years of your childhood and ask yourself what kinds of messages you got about wishing and wanting.

- Did your parents encourage your dreams?

- Did they try to suppress you and keep you in check?

- How did your family culture deal with competition?

I remember my own household very vividly in this regard. Most of the members of my family were very practical in their own way. They would have said they were "reality-based," in that the demands of living determined what they were allowed to want. My father was rather depressed and therefore had very few creative ideas. He had cut himself off from creative thinking long ago, through a kind of hopeless attitude. If he did get an urge or a desire for something, he seldom had the energy to do anything about it. My mother was so anxious that every new idea or dream was a cause of worry for her.

So I was set down in this family with all kinds of ideas and energy, and my parents did not know what to do with me. I'm sure I drove them nuts with my crazy schemes. In fact, I know so, because they told me often.

As you analyze your family culture, be aware of good and bad influences—and remember, it is hard to classify many influences as completely good or bad. For example, it was good for me in some ways that my parents were so reserved and skeptical. It taught me I had to prove my ideas before they would be accepted. Since my parents did not think everything their darling son did was wonderful, I was not stuck with a tendency to dream and want things that are impossible. On the other hand, I know there are times when I need encouragement to believe in myself and what I want.

Another important point about family structure is that what happened to you as a child may not be of prime importance. What is important is how you reacted to what happened. The way you took the psychological environments of your childhood and translated them into belief systems and actions is the key to understanding your patterns and deciding if they are functional or dysfunctional for you today.

Dream Bigger Dreams

To move our lives ahead, we need to have a dream. Great leaders down through the centuries have been people who had some kind of dream and the courage to see it through. So make your dreams a little bigger than usual. Push the envelope a bit and move strongly into the outer world all the images and ideas you have been harboring inside.

You will be amazed at what comes out once you start wielding your will.

Amplify and encourage your wants and desires. This step may take some spadework. Your goal here is to emphasize something you may have a great desire to hide. If you have a lot of prohibitions about wielding your will in the world, this could be a difficult assignment. You may feel domineering, selfish, insensitive—forced to confront a whole host of negative self-images. But I am going to ask you to push through them and try something different.

Every time you enter a room for a meeting or a class, I want you to immediately think about what you want to happen. How can you bring your personal leadership to the situation in a positive way? So often we just show up for things in life, never really thinking how we could affect the outcome.

Try to rise above that. What do you want to happen here? Maybe it will be to your advantage, maybe not. It's possible that what you want will help everybody. Exaggerating the desired outcome can help you amplify the wants and desires that have been there all along.

No matter how much our desires are pushed down or drummed out of us, they usually remain in some small way, somewhere, waiting to be revived. We can take a lesson from nature in this regard. As I mentioned earlier in the chapter on flow, I often spend time clearing brush from my property when I am in the country. This is stuff that has grown up where it obviously "wanted" to be. I love the look of things when I am done, but I realize that what I am doing is just temporary. Maybe next year, maybe ten years from now, what I have just cut down so carefully will be back again, and will go on to increase in size!

Meeting Power

I once confessed to a friend that I did not know what to do about an impending business meeting. A delicate situation was involved, and it was unclear who had authority. I said that I did not want to just waltz in and take over.

But my friend wisely said, "In every situation there is a certain amount of power present. You can grab most of it, or a little piece of it, but you can rest assured that someone at that meeting will go after it. It might as well be you!"

Exercise

Think of a recent situation that did not go the way you wanted.

- What role did you play?

- How did you feel going in?

- What family prejudices from the former exercise made things difficult for you?

- How would you have liked to handle the situation?

- What could you do in the future to improve things?

Our wants and desires can be slowed down or thwarted, but almost never completely erased. They are part of a deep root system, like my woods. They have a life of their own, and when frustrated they often go underground and resurface at a later date when the time is right. We can be glad that we are built this way too. Amplification will make our wishes known.

Take some small steps. Like the friend I mentioned earlier, many people get stuck at the point of taking action. They have no trouble *believing* they should be allowed to have big dreams, and they have little problem allowing themselves to spin those dreams lavishly—often describing them to friends and colleagues. But they never take action on them!

There are many reasons for this. Many people claim that they cannot get started on the "big" things, the dreams that are most important to them, because the size of the undertaking overwhelms them. Since dreams by their very nature are big and are often projected far out into the future, many steps need to be taken before they will be even partially realized. Therefore I believe one of the most important steps for accomplishing our dreams—turning them into reality—is to break them down into smaller parts.

Realize that every step in the right direction is much better than nothing at all. As an example, for some time now I have had the dream of getting back to a more artistic life. Besides the piano playing I do, I love to paint and create sculpture. Over the years I have allowed myself a few projects on the grounds of my house, creating some very simple sculptures. I have even completed a few paintings.

Dream Big Dreams

If, in the end, your wishes are too big, or your dreams and desires are unrealistic, don't worry. The world will help you take care of that. My experience is that we don't dream enough, or our wishes are much punier than our potential.

At Marble Collegiate Church in New York City, where I am privileged to be both a teacher and worshiper, members of the clergy staff often say that God has bigger dreams for us than we have for ourselves. This is another way of saying that the world is much larger and has much more potential than we ever can use; we just need to connect to it better.

Our wants and desires can help us do that. Remember what Auntie Mame said in the musical *Mame:* "Life is a banquet, and most of you suckers are starving to death!"

Recently I cleared a space in one of the outbuildings of my country house to serve as a studio, and I went down to Canal Street in New York City to get some supplies. I haven't done anything yet in this new space, but I know it is coming! Soon I will be working in there on a regular basis. How do I know? Just because I know I want to, and I have been observing myself taking the small steps that will get me there.

Break Dreams Down

Our biggest dreams can be quite intimidating. That's what my friend Ken said about writing his first book. But when he broke the project down into smaller steps, he got the job done.

Even the biggest ideas and projects are made of smaller elements. When we can break them down into smaller, doable steps, we begin to see success loom before us.

What Deer Know About Dreams

Recently I watched a deer sniffing around one of my rhododendron bushes. As you might know, this is a plant highly coveted by munching deer. I flew out the door and chased the deer up the ravine behind my house until it was just out of sight. Then I waited on the porch for a while. The deer eyed me cautiously from a distance, and then it feigned indifference and started grazing around another area. I went back into the house, but just for fun I watched from a window over the next half hour as the deer relentlessly took one small step at a time back to the object of his desire. Sure enough, after much meandering and stealthy stepping, the deer was back at work at his favorite site. My shooing him away was a temporary restraining order; he knew he would be back in time.

If deer keep working toward their dreams, we should too.

You might be surprised to find that you have a whole host of projects like this: great ideas you have not followed through on, just waiting there for the first step. If so, taking small steps might be the most important idea you take away from this chapter.

One Bite at a Time

Many great ideas never get started for want of the will to overcome that first initial resistance.

With apologies to my vegetarian friends, how do you eat a cow? One bite at a time.

Perhaps the intimidation of writing that first page or putting the first brush stroke on a canvas keeps you from starting. The first step really is the most difficult, since inertia is not just a principle of physics but built into the human condition.

Exercise

Is there a particular wish or project that you know you have always wanted to do? Pick one that is big and bothersome, and break it down into some initial small steps just to get it started. These steps can be so small as to seem insignificant. The only requirement is that each element takes you one step closer to accomplishment. The size of the step does not matter.

You may not even know it, but you have probably been taking small steps toward your dream all along—possibly for years. Perhaps you have always wanted to take a trip to Italy, but never thought you could. If you scan the fabric of your life, you may well notice that things Italian pop up quite a bit. I'll bet you have gone to more than your share of Italian restaurants. You have probably picked up a few Italian phrases. And likely you have gone to an Italian movie or two. If you do a thorough search, you may see that you have already been preparing actively for a trip to Italy. Often, on a subconscious level, we find we are doing the preliminary work we need to reach our dreams.

Exercise

Go on, try it. Think of another of those pesky big dreams that have dogged you in your life. Scan everywhere, as if you were doing an Internet search, and discover the steps you have already taken. You will find many more tracks than you expect. Your will has already begun the trip toward your dream—all you need to do is follow.

Step back and look at the forest. It is great to take small steps toward your wishes and desires. There's a lot of satisfaction built into every one that moves you just a little farther along toward your dreams. It is also good from time to time to step back and see if all of your projects are really furthering your life in the way you want—toward your "big picture" and vision of where you want your life to go.

It's time to ask: "Where am I going? Where will these desires and wishes take me?" I truly believe that if you follow your will and do the things you want to do in life, eventually your big picture will emerge. I also believe you can really move things along if you are able to shift your focus from the trees to the forest and back again to the trees.

Some people say they are detail-oriented and do not have a broad vision of their lives. Others seem to focus only on the big picture and profess to have little ability to handle the details. I believe we have a natural proclivity for one or the other. I also believe that, whether we are temperamentally suited to seeing the forest or the trees, we can move toward our dreams more effectively when we "stretch" and learn to take the opposite outlook as well.

> ### Forest or Trees?
>
> I believe we can really move toward our dreams if we are able to shift our focus from the trees to the forest and back again to the trees.

In the Myers-Briggs Type Indicator®, this would correlate roughly to the difference between people who are "intuitive" and those who are "sensate."

- *Intuitives* are always looking far ahead, paying attention to the goal and seeing how all the pieces fit together to get them there.
- *Sensates* are focused on the details.

Both approaches are important and necessary. You can get there either way, but why not be in charge of both?

It can be unnecessarily limiting to classify ourselves as just detail or vision people. Just because one is our natural way does not mean we need to narrow ourselves to what comes naturally.

Exercise

Think of a situation where you are either hopelessly bogged down in details or so stuck on an overall vision that you don't know what to do. See if you can shift your focus. If the details are somewhat in hand, check to see if the whole thing is going anywhere. Conversely, if you know where you want to be eventually, consider what details you will have to organize in order to get the job done.

It is good to check in often on where you stand on the issue of focus. Doing so may cause you to shift your focus, or it may not. You may want to wait with the details for a while to see where they are leading. And you may want to hold the vision until the various details become clear.

Enjoy the process. One of the most enjoyable aspects of living is turning our wants and desires into reality. Whether they come sooner or later hardly matters in most cases. And some of the most satisfying wants are the ones that take the longest—that demand the most work.

In fact, some cherished wishes never come to fruition.

A friend of mine recently told me about a wise lesson he had learned from his teenage son. He and his wife had not selected a birthday present for him—and the birthday was only several days away. So my friend, who had no idea what to get, decided to interview him and find out what he wanted. My friend suggested several gifts, but nothing seemed to get the young man's approval. His son finally said, "You know, Dad. Sometimes wanting something is better than actually getting it!"

My friend was stunned to learn that his rather young son already knew something it had taken him many years to learn—something with which most of us can easily resonate. We have all had the experience of wanting something so badly for a time that when we finally got it, the possession of the desired object was a letdown.

A lot of the fun is in the wanting—and in the expectation and preparation of owning or trying something new. Whether we get what we wish for is really not always the issue. If we work toward something and it is granted, hopefully we will have the good grace to accept it and give ourselves credit for having brought it about.

Wanting Versus Having

No matter how ardently some of us want something or work toward having it, sometimes it just isn't destined to come about.

A friend of mine always loved antique automobiles. He went to car shows and subscribed to all the collector-car magazines. He dreamed of the day when he would be able to start collecting these cars, but that day was put off again and again.

Since he was not a wealthy man, much of what he made went into taking care of his family and just plain living. One day his wife bought him a scale model of one of his favorite cars.

Since that day, he now collects models. He still goes to car shows, and still gets those magazines. Interestingly, he enjoys the hobby as much as ever, but it is the knowledge he has gained about the cars, and the enjoyment of seeing them that is paramount. Owning them, he now reflects, is probably more trouble than it is worth.

The message is, goals can change. Sometimes by modifying them, we can still attain the satisfaction they promise.

If you really think back to many of the best things in your life, you may well see that the process of working toward a goal was often the best part. The rehearsals for the school play, the lessons at tennis camp, the design of your new office, and the shopping for that new boat are a part of the total experience, not just some process to get through.

> **Exercise**
>
> Think of another one of your dreams or major wishes. Are you enjoying the pursuit of this dream? Is the process itself fun? Or does it fill you with longing or self-disparagement? How could you make the pursuit of the dream as important as the dream itself?

Keep your will in perspective. Try not to let the way of the will be a tyrant that dominates your everyday existence. With patience, planning, and determination, many good things will come to you. Willing and wanting is not a passive process, but it is a very rewarding one.

The key is to exercise your will with care, self-knowledge, and, at times, an active sense of humor.

EXERCISES

You may have noticed that this chapter on will is structured slightly differently from the others in this book. The exercises and self-help tools are embodied within the chapter's text itself, rather than set aside at the end. This alternative structure is intended to help you, the reader, make positive changes regarding the way you wield your will at the same time as you are introduced to the larger, "big picture" principles of the chapter.

7 LIVE IN GRACE

I recently read a newspaper story about a woman who was living in a terrible neighborhood in New York City, trying to raise two sons. She was an honest, hardworking woman who was trying to create the best possible life for her children, despite the many hardships she faced.

She was a religious woman. Furthermore, she had put strong emphasis on books and learning in her household, and was very upset that the public schools around her were not able to provide her children with the kind of education she—and they—desired. Yet instead of giving up hope, she remained faithful and kept on striving.

Then she heard about a foundation that paid private school tuition for the children of deserving families, and she applied. Her two sons were accepted, and they will attend private school next year.

(Continued on next page.)

(Continued from previous page.)

This simple story—unremarkable on the surface—
serves as an ideal starting point for our exploration of
grace. For that woman was surely living in a state of
grace. Wonderful things had happened for her and her
sons. Yet these things had not come "out of the blue."
They were a result of a wonderful preparedness on
her part.

The woman lived well, rising above her circumstances. She set high standards for herself and others.
Her priorities grew from a strong value system. And
she never lost faith that things would become better if
she was willing, not to sit back passively and wait, but
to take action to reach her goals.

That's what grace is all about. It is a favored state in
which we are supported and buoyed by positive
forces—perhaps from God. Yet grace is not passive.
Through grace, we actively usher surprising new
blessings into our own lives.

L iving in a state of grace means living in a complete, whole, evolved way. It means enjoying life deeply, on a profound level. At the same time, it means living out the life that was intended for you.

WHAT IS GRACE?

Grace is the culmination of all the ideas, problems and solutions presented in the earlier chapters of this book. When you begin to live in grace, you become a person who:

- *Is not unsettled by chaos.* The graceful person lives peacefully in what other people perceive as chaotic settings, content to observe and wait for larger processes to unfold.
- *Does not worry excessively about luck.* The graceful person is not preoccupied with false concerns of luck and unluck, but is intrigued with observing larger processes as they reveal their real shape and import.
- *Lives in a state of flow.* The graceful person playfully allows inspiration and energies to infuse all of life's activities and processes.
- *Moves life ahead by making decisions.* The graceful person makes value-based choices that lead to authentic, rewarding outcomes in life.

- *Masters karma.* The graceful person finds positive ways to contribute good acts to the world—and also reaps the benefits that karma brings back.

- *Lives willfully.* The graceful person makes a personal and long-lasting contribution to other people and the world by acting decisively.

Grace imparts other benefits as well, since the graceful person is also:

- *Sensate and sensual.* The graceful person lives in a state of sensate awareness and openness to life, people, and the messages they bring.

- *Exquisitely active.* The graceful person is fully involved in life on every level—enjoying life, living fully, leaving a mark on the world and serving as an inspiration and beacon to others.

Grace is a unique and blessed state of experience. It is a higher, more evolved way of living our lives. When we are able to live in grace, our inner selves are engaged in a beneficial, continuous interplay with the outer world. We sense that our needs and desires will be heeded and met by God or some higher power. In some mystical and wonderful way, we are partnering with "someone" or "something" that we often do not understand completely.

Grace is not passive. We don't sit idly back as all kinds of good things happen to us. Grace requires our participation and our work. In grace, we partner with higher forces to create our own blessed state of mind. Good things come to us, because:

- We are prepared for good things to happen. We have worked and made our lives ready for the gifts we will receive.

- We are aware. Without the right kind of thinking and awareness, we can miss the gifts that come to us from grace. Many people receive considerable gifts in life, and hardly notice. Graceful people live in the opportunity.

So in grace, we are living fully, in an extremely positive way.

Grace and Karma

In what way is grace different from karma, which we explored at length earlier in this book? Karma and its positive returns are part of grace, it is true. Yet at the most basic, karma is more mechanistic than grace. In karma, we cause good things to come into our lives by taking positive actions in the world. In karma, we shape the content of our lives by our actions.

In contrast, grace is more *internal*. It is a state of mind that invites a higher power into our lives. Through anticipation, awareness and a profound appreciation of life, we open up and accept the good things that life holds in store.

Amazing Grace

The words of the old hymn tell us:

"Amazing grace, how sweet the sound . . ."

Grace comes to good people who have prepared and done their work, who live according to high standards, and who actively anticipate the arrival of wonderful things in their lives.

CHAPTER SEVEN

Religious Conceptions of Grace

If you said the word "grace" to a small group of people, chances are that many of them would respond, "Oh, yes, grace—that's a Christian concept, isn't it?"

Indeed it is. Grace—meaning a blessed state of happiness—is often mentioned by Christians. For fundamentalist Christians, the concept of grace intermingles with the notion of salvation. By accepting Christ as a savior, they feel, they have freed themselves from sin and empowered themselves to live an eternal life.

"Changed into His Likeness . . ."

And we all, with unveiled faces, beholding the glory of the Lord, are being changed into his likeness from one degree of glory to another.

—Corinthians

What better way to describe the experience of recognizing the reality that grace can be made part of our lives? Through grace, we accept the presence of the divine within.

I like to think of grace in a somewhat different way. Grace is a Christian concept because Jesus lived in such a *gracious,* evolved way. Jesus was fully immersed in living. He truly connected to his life, elevating himself and those around him. He sacrificed and suffered cruelly for the things he believed. In other words, he strived to receive blessings and gifts, not by living passively, but by raising his experience to the very highest levels—even in troubling, trying, and painful ways.

Taken in this way, grace is not a Christian concept per se, or even a religious concept. *Grace is a state that can be achieved by all people of all faiths.* It is about a way of living, not about participation in any one religion or belief system. Grace can be anyone's—and it can be yours—for the asking.

THE CHANGING FACE OF GRACE

In the earliest days of Christianity, grace was interpreted as a state that could be achieved by abstinence from sin—even as a state that served as an antidote to sin. Here are only a few landmarks along the road paved by the great Christian thinkers and theologians who considered the question of grace:

St. Augustine (354–430), possibly the most important philosopher and theologian of early Christianity, considered grace at length in his *Confessions* and *City of God.* He was striving to reconcile Christian dogma with Platonic and other classical philosophies—a daunting undertaking, to say the least. Augustine saw grace as a defining aspect of the Christian experience.

St. Thomas Aquinas (c. 1225–1274), an Italian Dominican theologian, also dealt with issues of grace by striving to rationalize Christianity with the classical ideals of Greek and Arab thought. His synthesis of faith and reason stands as a major achievement of medieval theology.

Martin Luther (1483–1546) was, of course, the founder of the Protestant Reformation. He really struggled with his faith. Before he chose to break away from the Church of Rome, he entered a monastery, was ordained in 1507, and struggled with the grace of God. Upon emerging into the world, he tacked those famous 95 theses on the door of the church in Wittenberg, saying that the grace of God should be available to all people, since the monasticism of his day was not doing the trick. (It was then believed that the presence of religious orders was sufficient to bring the grace of God to all people. Luther said no—something more direct was needed.)

The debate over the nature of grace has hardly diminished in the last few centuries. In more recent times, it has been taken up by Karl Barth (1886–1968) and Paul Tillich (1886–1965), two of the most influential Christian theologians of our century.

Is Grace Eminent or Immanent?

To my mind, one of the most interesting conundrums about grace—one that has been argued for years—is the question of eminence versus immanence.

The concept of an eminent grace holds that grace comes from "out there" somewhere. It rains down on us from God, from the stars, or from some "other" place. We humans need to passively wait for it to fall on us and bestow its gifts. There is not much we can do to invite it into our lives.

The concept of an immanent grace holds that grace is already present in each of us. It exists in our souls. By recognizing and accepting the *imago dei* (literally, "image of God" or "face of God") that already exists within each of us, we can live in grace.

As Jesus said, "The kingdom of God is within you."

I choose to believe that grace is immanent and eminent. In fact, such a concept of grace is central to the views I present in this chapter. I believe there is an image of God in each of us that can come out when we live an authentic life. But I also believe that grace—like things—happens to us.

Being Receptive to Grace

If grace is already resident—immanent—in each of us, why do so many people find it so difficult to achieve? There are two important reasons.

Lack of awareness. If people are unaware that grace is within them, waiting to open, it is all but impossible for them to find it. Learning that grace is there—that is an option that each of us can choose to exercise—is the first step toward moving our lives into this higher state.

"I never knew anything about happiness or living in grace," says a man who transformed his life through a 12-step program. "I simply never knew it was an option until someone told me."

The Psalmist Writes of Grace

Cease to dwell on days gone by, and to brood over past history. Here and now I will do a new thing. This moment, it will break from the bud. Can you perceive it?

— Isaiah 43

These moving words speak to us on an immanent grace—one that is already present within each of us, waiting to emerge.

A negative outlook. People who resolutely refuse to admit the possibility that good things might happen in their lives are cutting themselves off from any possibility of grace. In a sense, they have resigned themselves to a second-class existence.

For several years, I had a counseling client who came in each week and complained about everything in his life. The people with whom he worked were slow and stupid, he told me. His wife was a "griper" who complained all the time. His children were not responsible or accomplished. His possessions never made him happy or met his expectations. When I suggested to him that things might not be as bad as he claimed, and that he should look on the brighter side, he told me I was naive. Finally, he stopped showing up for our counseling sessions and left in disgust. He didn't even pay my last bill!

Now, this man was well-to-do and accomplished. He had a life that many people would envy. His story shows that people can resist grace and the happiness it brings, no matter how good their lives may be.

If you have an attitude that says nothing good will ever happen to you, then you have created your own future through a powerful—and very negative—self-fulfilling prophecy. By accepting the good, you begin to expand your life into remarkable new vistas.

Why Invite Grace into Your Life?

The answers to that question are nearly obvious. Yet before we go into techniques for bringing grace into your life, I think it might be a good idea to take a closer look at the whys that stand behind that decision.

By living in a state of grace, you will:

- Be happier in your life, work, and human relationships.
- Enjoy more success, because you will be tapping a deep inner well of focused energy.
- Positively affect the lives of other people. People who live in a joyous, gracious way invariably bring the state of grace to the lives of other people as well. They become leaders who elevate all those around them.

Graceful Grace

One beautiful day I was taking a walk along the East River in Manhattan. There were hundreds of people out there, having a great time.

I ended up watching a pickup basketball game that involved about 20 men.

There were young kids, middle-agers, people of all races. Some of the players looked like investment bankers from Wall Street; others looked like high school kids. In the midst of them, there was one guy who was really in tune with the game. Everywhere he went, the ball was there. Every time he got anywhere near the basket, the ball went in. I've never seen such beautiful movement.

- Enjoy the benefits of karma, luck, flow, and all the other positive forces described in this book. Grace is the unifying force that both emanates from them and underlies them.

- Live a more fulfilling and spiritual life. Whether you are avowedly religious or not, grace allows you to live in a more spiritual, exhilarating way. You will be leading your life in unity with a higher force.

By opening the grace within you, you are accepting the presence of a strong "life partner." That acceptance will make each step of your life journey lighter, happier, and filled with ease.

CHAPTER SEVEN

HOW TO MAKE GRACE PART OF YOUR JOURNEY

As I mentioned above, you have already taken the first step—
and possibly the most important one—toward making grace
part of your life. By reading this book and this chapter, you
have become aware of the fact that grace is an option in your
life. Grace can now open up for you.

Here are some potent strategies, built on that foundation,
that can make grace not just a hoped-for experience, but an
integral part of your life journey.

Become better attuned to life's hidden messages. A
great deal has been written on the subject of *synchronicity*—
which means, literally, "at the same time." In my view, synchronicity is a phenomenon that occurs when *something in the
outer world happens at the same time that something happens in
the soul.* Sometimes, such events can be quite dramatic.

Consider this story of Freud and Jung having one of their
famed conversations together. Freud had picked Jung to be
his successor, yet there Jung sat, telling Freud that he was
about to part ways with a key psychological precept—Freud's
insistence that the unconscious mind was centered on the
Oedipus complex.

Just as the conversation was at its most heated, a loud
noise—like wood splitting—filled the room. The two men
got up and, sure enough, a large bookshelf had suddenly
cracked wide open. Its wood had been sitting there drying,
getting ready to split for decades, yet it picked that exact
moment to imitate the rift that was taking place between the
two pioneering psychologists and their views of the psyche.

Of course, not all such events in our lives are quite so dramatic. Most of them are quite subtle. If we are not aware and
on the lookout, we run the risk of missing them entirely.
Something not quite as dramatic—but just as remarkable—
once happened to a friend of mine named Johanna.

When Johanna was a girl, she was given a beautiful ring that had been passed down from her grandmother. It was a fine little gold ring and it had a pearl in it. One day she was playing with her best friend, and the two little girls noticed that they were both wearing rings.

Johanna's friend's ring was quite different from her own. It was made of bright red plastic, and it had some cheerful-looking fruit painted on it. The two little girls made a pact of friendship. They consecrated their friendship by having a little ceremony and exchanging rings.

When the two girls got home that evening and told of the friendship ceremony, their parents quickly arranged for a reswap of the rings. They explained their actions to the girls as best they could—that the rings were not of equal value, that one was an heirloom. The girls agreed to remain good friends, even without the exchange of rings.

As Johanna entered her twenties, she embarked on a close relationship with a man she really cared about. They were thinking of getting married. She had a job that required her to travel, and she often attended conferences. At one of them, she met a man who seemed very attractive—the proverbial "tall, dark stranger" who could sweep her off her feet. An affair was in the wind. And Johanna was really interested, flattered, and tempted.

But on the day the conference was to end, she reached down into her pocketbook to look for some change or her keys and found instead that little ring from her childhood. She did not even know it was in her purse. Somehow, it was just sitting there. Johanna sat down in the hotel lobby and said to herself, "I'm going to do it again. I'm going to swap something of great permanent value for something that's only inferior and temporary."

So she stood up and left the conference and didn't have that affair.

That, I think, was a moment of grace. But it could have been lost if Johanna had not been aware and looking for it—if she had not been attuned to the little unexpected messages life was placing in her path.

Messages are all around us. If we strive to stay open and aware, life will consistently yield to us the messages we need to hear—messages of insight and grace.

Try to become more comfortable with ambiguities in day-to-day events. It takes work and concentration, yet it is possible to suspend judgment as we move from day to day and activity to activity. As noted at length in an earlier chapter, we can delude ourselves by constantly applying the terms "lucky" and "unlucky" to daily events. So too can we deceive ourselves by applying the judgmental values of "good" or "bad."

A successful businessman I know sums up the benefits of accepting ambiguities this way: "Last week I had to make a very difficult phone call to let our accountant of ten years know we would no longer be giving him our business. Another accountant had come along—one who had extensive experience with businesses like ours, and who had already shown us just how much he could save us on taxes.

"The day before I had to make that call, I was tied up in knots. I kept telling myself, 'This is going to be really, really bad.'

"Well, I made the call, and it was not bad. In fact, my accountant told me that he was just about to call us to let us know that he would no longer be dealing with firms like ours. He had decided to specialize. What promised to be a bad conversation ended up being very cordial and positive."

So it was, too, with a single woman I know who developed quite a crush on a man in her community. Through careful planning over a period of months, she managed to meet him. She engaged him in several conversations. Finally, she got up the gumption to ask him to accompany her to a Broadway show.

"Boy, was I looking forward to that date!" she recalls. "I shopped for the right dress. I got a haircut. It was going to be great! But it was a disaster. We had nothing in common. He actually seemed unattractive to me by the end of the evening. We parted friends, but I saw that anticipating good things in an unrealistic way can be the most effective way to cause something bad to happen."

When we suspend judgment about events and just live them, we come closer to the coveted goal of "living in the moment." We become better attuned to the messages grace is sending us, because we gain the leeway to judge later whether the happenings of our lives have been positive, negative, or somewhere in between.

Don't Let Your Problems Become Your Future

If your life is not in the best place these days—if you are fighting a major problem—it may be tempting to assume that grace will have to be postponed. Well, not really. Grace is something that can be claimed, even by people in the direst circumstances imaginable.

The quality of people's lives is often astounding, even in poverty. And history teaches us that many great women and men in history—the greatest achievers of any age—started their lives in very disadvantageous circumstances.

So I'd urge you to start doing the work you need to do to claim grace—no matter what challenges are currently "on your plate."

You have nothing to lose, and a world to gain.

Strive to connect with your true self. Most of us have developed various personas that accompany us through life. In social situations, we present ourselves in certain ways. At work or in business settings, we adopt a different character. When we are courting a love partner, we adopt yet another persona and wear it like an attractive new dress or suit of clothes. Humans, it seems, are akin to chameleons.

Even when we are alone, in our quiet moments, we can easily slip into personas as quickly as we slip into well-worn slippers. In our solitary hours, some of us become mired in thinking about the past. Or we dwell on perceived slights and wrongs we have suffered or lapse into self-aggrandizing fantasies.

Beneath all those other personas and adopted personalities lies something deeper, more profound. *It is the true self.* By connecting with this authentic self, we invite grace into our lives. Grace, in fact, enters into our lives through our true selves.

My dear friend Ken Ruge wrote these insightful words about the true self in his book *Where Do I Go from Here?* (McGraw-Hill, 1998):

> What is your true self? Essentially, the true self is a mystery and if I could tell you, I would let you know. It's that special voice we use when we talk to ourselves—the internal voice that's underneath all the other voices. It's the "me" who you talk to and the "me" who you are.

Seeking out your true self requires time and patience. On the subject of finding the true self, Ken also wrote in *Where Do I Go from Here?*

> In a way, the true self is a little like those Russian Matushka dolls. In searching for it, you discover one

doll and find that there is another one, and another one, and still another level to explore. There is an unfolding quality to the search. It is a search that takes time and cultivation (intentional effort) because the true self is essentially incomplete . . . There is an important place here for waiting, for gestation, for incubation, for respecting the movement of hidden processes. You can't set a deadline by which time you will have pinpointed your true inner self.

How can you find your true self? There are no easy ways, but here are some ideas that may work for you.

- *Make friends with your "inner voice."* Spend some time alone each day, simply thinking your thoughts and listening to them. A quiet place in your home can be a great boon to this process. You need a quiet, peaceful place to connect with yourself and your inner self.

- *Keep a journal.* Many people report that they gain new understanding of themselves through the writing process itself—and then again by reading their own written thoughts in the days and weeks afterward.

- *Engage in pursuits that hold meaning for you.* I find that machines hold a real significance for me. Give me a broken machine—anything from a clock to a lawnmower—and I can usually pull it apart, analyze the problem and repair it. In so doing, I learn something about myself. I seem to become engaged in a pure process in which all my personas—the social and so on—fall away. Stripped free of them, I feel that I have encountered something true about myself, if only for a few moments.

Fits and Starts

Carl Jung once said that the way to wholeness is "through fitful starts and wrong turnings."

So too is the search for the true self.

We're going to make many mistakes and wrong turns in our journeys through life. Yet with the right outlook, every one of those turns can bring us closer to a connection with our inner, true selves—the place where grace dwells.

Direct positive expectations toward your life. When you expect wonderful things to happen, you increase the chances that they really will. "I have seen this work time and time again," says an entrepreneur I know. "When I believe a deal is going to work—when I expect it to happen—its success becomes almost a foregone conclusion. There's no more 'selling,' just the working out of details."

A commodities broker shares this insight: "When I start the day feeling that things are going to go well, they usually do. When I start out feeling that the day will be a bust, it almost always is. Statistically speaking, a positive outlook yields great returns for me. It makes me conclude that there really is something to all the talk about positive thinking."

I'll be the first to admit that the reasons behind this principle are mysterious. But the fact is, positive expectations usually yield positive outcomes, just as negative expectations yield negative.

Be brave, take action, and do what needs to be done. Curiously, you can invite a state of grace into your life by tackling problems and issues directly—even problems that are daunting and unpleasant. When you move such problems out of the center of your consciousness, you "roll the road-blocks away." You make new space for the positive influence of grace to enter your life.

There are many instances when doing the brave or the difficult leads to a state of elation as blockages are removed from our lives. I once worked with a wonderful woman who had been experiencing anxiety attacks with increasing frequency. She could function pretty well most of the time—get to work and get to her temple—but there were many other times when she was simply not able to function.

How Do You Know When Grace Is "Working"?

At a seminar I gave some months ago, a man in the audience asked, "How do you know when you've achieved a sense of grace? How can you be sure you're not just on a roll or having a good day?"

That's a very good question. Two important differences between grace and momentary happiness:

Depth. In grace, we feel a sense of deep, caring support, and belonging. As one man says, "I feel I've come home again."

Duration. In grace, we feel that support from day to day, through good times and through bad.

Of course, there is nothing wrong with just being happy. But grace is more long-lasting and more profound—it's literally "something else."

CHAPTER SEVEN

As we worked on her emotional blockage, we finally saw that it was tied to a very specific problem with her father. Now, her father was head of a family business in which she and several other family members were employed. At 86 years old, he was still guardian of the company, going to work every day of the week.

The problem was, her father was beginning to lose the ability to run the company, and the rest of the family was suffering because of it. He was forgetting important business routines, making impulsive decisions that the rest of the family did not agree with, and upsetting everyone from his own children to the people who worked in the mail room.

My client, especially, was suffering from the situation. As the only child of her father in the business, it fell to her to tell him it was time to step down. She loved her father and dreaded the encounter. Finally, she got up the nerve to sit quietly and lovingly with him and explain kindly and gently that it was time to let other people take over conducting the business from day to day.

Interestingly, her father was ready to hear this difficult news. Even though there were some tense moments during that conversation and in the days afterward, both she and her father felt they had done very well in discussing and overcoming the problem.

Her anxiety attacks did go away, incidentally. They've been replaced by the positive, goal-oriented anxiety that comes from running a business. But, as she puts it, "I am now in my glory days. Things are better than I ever anticipated." Unless this woman had gotten the nerve to bravely do what she needed to do, her life would have remained blocked—and her sense of stifling panic would have almost certainly continued to rise. Now, it seems that grace is showering down all around her and she is living the life she deserves.

A Short Course in Grace

I like to define grace this way: "Living your life in anticipation of something wonderful."

Simple words—yet they have the power to orient your life in a new kind of way, if you really think about them and make them yours.

Have hope and faith in God and the future. That can be a tall order, of course! Yet with the right outlook, we can learn to trust that good things are coming our way. We can even learn to trust in God.

My colleague and respected friend Dr. Arthur Caliandro, head minister of Marble Collegiate Church in New York, often sums up the essence of his spiritual life with these simple words: "Trust, and then trust some more." In a sense, he is recommending that we relinquish control over our problems—give them over to some higher power. And he is right.

In an extraordinary way, we invite grace into our lives when we admit that our problems and issues are bigger than we are and that we need grace to help solve them.

Take your place in a church, temple, or other caring community. A sense of grace is catching. When like-minded people who care for each other come together and unite around a common goal—whether it be worship, running a company, or playing a sport—the reality of grace is more likely to enter and grow stronger.

Praying for Rain

I like to use the expression, "Never pray for rain without a hoe in your hand." In other words, life brings to us pretty much what we expect and ask for.

Ask for the good, and grace stands ready to help you find it. Ask for the bad—or let the bad color your view of the world—and life will accommodate you too, by giving you a bad time.

We really do get what we ask for. We become what we think. Given the choice, ask for the good. It is within our power to ask for, and receive, the higher kind of life that comes through grace.

EXERCISES

1. **Direct extremely positive expectations at some task that lies before you.** The task you choose could be any that you sense will be difficult or trying. For example:

   — Approaching a lending institution to present a business plan and ask for funding.

   — Applying for a job.

   — Talking to your spouse or partner about a problem that you have been reluctant to discuss before.

   — Starting an exercise program or diet.

   The list might go on and on. But in the days before you perform the task you have selected, try to direct very positive beliefs and expectations toward it. Begin by envisioning how the encounter might play out if it went particularly well. If you are going to a job interview, for instance—and that is your task of choice—create a scenario in which you meet a kind, supportive interviewer who is impressed by your credentials.

Bring a prodigious amount of energy and enthusiasm to the task. Then visualize an ideal outcome. For example, you complete a sterling interview and, three days later, are offered the job.

Taking these steps is a good way to invite grace into your life. More important, you will probably find that your positive expectations lead to just the outcome you envisioned. Grace will already be working for you—and when it is, it is likely to continue to do so.

2. **"Turn up" your appreciation for the good things in your life.** Instead of taking the good things in your life—your family, spouse, home, work, and all the rest—for granted, start to appreciate them actively.

Begin to make statements like these:

— "Thank God I have this wonderful job that I enjoy so much."

— "I am so glad I live in a country that provides me and my family with safety and security."

— "My husband has seen me through some very difficult times, and I appreciate him deeply."

As you move your appreciation from the passive state into the active, you will find much more than a brightening of your mood. You will also gain a glimpse of grace and open the door for a new range of surprising blessings.

3. **Share your newfound grace with someone else.** You can do this exercise with a good friend, your spouse, a trusted mentor, or anyone who means a

great deal to you. You needn't go to that person and say, "I have discovered the power of grace in my life." (Of course you *could,* if you feel your confidant would understand.) Simply set aside some time with that other person and make statements like these:

— "There have been some wonderful things happening in my life."

— "I feel as though all the hard work I've been doing for years is finally beginning to pay off."

— "My kids are bringing me such joy. Here's what they've been up to lately. . ."

Don't be too surprised if that important other person reciprocates, telling his or her own stories of blessings and positive events. Through this exercise you will notice that grace is cumulative. When you share it with someone else, your excitement and elation builds to the point where grace is not an abstract principle. It becomes palpable in your life.

4. **Declare that you are living in a state of grace—a new, higher place.** The words you choose to make this declaration are, of course, up to you. Still, they might fall along these lines:

— "I feel that it has finally happened. I sense the presence of God in my everyday life. I am no longer going it alone."

— "For the first time in my life, I feel uplifted and supported by some positive force. I am no longer going it alone."

— "The power to do whatever I want to do with my life is finally mine. I am supporting God and the universe, and they are supporting me too."

— "Through grace, I have mastered luck, chaos, and other unruly forces that once seemed to control me. I am now at the helm of my own life's ship."

Such statements serve as a seal upon the state of grace, legitimizing it and making it part of your experience in life. They serve as an uplifting, empowering acknowledgment that you have left your old life behind and entered into something higher and new.

Those words also serve as a fitting call to action as you end this chapter and start your new life.

EPILOGUE: A SEVEN-STEP ACTION PLAN TO TAKE CONTROL OF YOUR LIFE

As the preceding pages have shown, you can exert far more control over your life than you may have imagined—and wield far more control over your destiny. I hope that the exercises accompanying each chapter have helped you get your life moving forward: seeing chaos for what it is, taking more control over luck, mastering the art of getting in flow, and making other important life changes as well.

Yet I feel that more work is still needed. The fact is, even when we have completed the work already laid out in this book, *we can still get in our own way.* As I like to say, we can fall victim to "self-imposed destinies."

What does that mean? In brief: *A self-imposed destiny is a highly personalized version of a self-fulfilling prophecy.* If you recall conversations you've had with people over the years, chances are you have glimpsed the outlines of self-imposed destinies.

- "I know I'm overweight," my friend Jacqueline reports, "but everyone in my family has always been heavy, so it's part of my genetic makeup."
- "I'm lonely," says Doug, a man who came to me for counseling. "But I've always been shy, and shy people have fewer friends than other people. People like me are just happier by themselves."
- "My job is deadly dull," says Chris, a man I helped through some vocational counseling. "But it provides a steady income for me and my family. And isn't work supposed to be *work,* after all? If it was meant to be fun, they would call it *fun,* right?"

I've chosen quotes from Jacqueline, Doug, and Chris for a reason. They are people who have spent years battling three quite common life challenges:

- Losing weight.
- Overcoming shyness and making friends.
- Making career changes.

Even if you are not facing exactly the same challenges yourself, you will find that the lessons they learned in moving *their* lives ahead will help you gain perspective on your own process of change. As we review the Seven-Step Process for Taking Control of Your Life in the following pages, we'll return to these three people as object lessons at each step along the way.

Keep in mind that the process we are about to examine takes up only a few pages in this book. This is somewhat deceptive, because completing it *takes time.* In fact, I would encourage you to devote *a great deal of time* to the process. Work on one step for a few hours, then walk away from it for a day or two. And then return to it. After all, you will be uncovering and confronting deep-seated self-beliefs and limitations. They need some time to emerge—and even more time to change.

With these preliminaries out of the way, let's embark on a path of meaningful change.

The Seven-Step Action Plan for Taking Control of Your Life.

Step 1: Analyze Your Life

Step 2: Examine Your Attitude

Step 3: Set Goals for Key Change Areas

Step 4: Get Going on Your Goals

Step 5: Examine Your Resistance

Step 6: Take Courage

Step 7: Enjoy the Fruits of Your Effort

STEP 1: ANALYZE YOUR LIFE

The goal of Step 1 is to uncover areas where you feel unfulfilled and stalled—areas where you would make some real progress if you became motivated and began to move your life forward. Of course, you need to analyze the good things you have in your life and to be thankful for them. But for the purposes of this exercise, I'd like you to concentrate on something else: *Areas in your life where you feel dissatisfied and where you feel you don't have enough control.*

EPILOGUE

I encourage you to examine any and all areas of your life where you feel dissatisfied or unfulfilled. At the same time, I urge you to take a particularly close look at three vital areas, since they often harbor life's greatest dissatisfactions:

Your relationship to friends and loved ones. Are you happy in your relationships? In the way you connect with people? With the amount of contact you have? With the social aspects of your life? In sum, are you feeling fulfilled, and as close to people as you would like to feel?

As you consider this important area, first examine your *closest* relationships with your spouse and family members. Then move out into your "next circle" and examine your relationships to close friends. Then move outward one more "circle" by considering how fulfilled you feel in your more casual contacts with people you work with or know from daily routines.

Your work and job. Perform a similar analysis on your working life. How are you relating to your job? Do you really like it? Is it something you are just putting up with and tolerating—or even something you actively hate? Do you like to go to work each day or do you resist? On a more subtle level, are there aspects of your work that you like and others that you dislike?

What do your answers to these questions tell you about how fulfilled you are in your work? Do they lead you to believe you should be making some needed changes?

Your hopes and dreams. What have you accomplished that you are proud of and happy about? At your age, have you achieved everything you thought you would? Are there goals that have eluded you totally? Are there hopes and dreams that life has beaten you down on? These are important questions to answer as you focus in on areas of your life where change is needed and overdue.

Before we move on to Step 2, let's check in with Jacqueline, Doug, and Chris to see what they discovered as they completed Step 1.

- "I realized that I was still dreaming about getting my life in order and losing weight," says Jacqueline. "I've all but given up hope of ever making it happen but, yes, it is still the unreachable dream I hold closest to my heart."

- "I realized that there's a difference between being *resigned* to being lonely and being *happy* with being lonely," says Doug, "and also that I am not happy at all about spending my life alone. If I don't do something to correct the situation, I will probably spend the next two or three decades feeling like a second-class, lonely person."

- "Would I like an exciting job?" asks Chris. "Of course. Wouldn't we all? But I think that I had just resigned myself to the impossibility of ever finding one. In this step, I realized I would still like more excitement and fulfillment in my work, even though I had long suppressed such desires."

STEP 2: EXAMINE YOUR ATTITUDE

Take a realistic, close look at your attitude in the key areas you uncovered in Step 1. Why are attitudes important? Because, through our attitudes, we either limit ourselves and remain stuck where we are—*or we give ourselves permission to change and move ahead.* If we can confront and change the attitudes that hold us back, we empower ourselves to make the changes we need to make in our lives.

As you try to uncover limiting attitudes—a process requiring patience and time—take a close look at these important areas:

Familial attitudes and beliefs. Most of us live with family-based expectations that exert a limiting influence on our lives. You have heard them described by friends or acquaintances. Often they emerge in statements like these:

> "We're just not a money-making family. We're right in the middle of the middle class, and we don't have the money knack."

> "I come from a long line of couch potatoes. We're not an exercising kind of clan. We *watch* sports, we don't *do* sports."

> "We've always lived in the Midwest. We're Midwesterners. No way I could have gone to college out east."

You might even have heard something more extreme, in the form of statements like these:

> "We never get a break."

> "Our family is unlucky."

> "We're marked for tragedy."

Negative personal limitations and beliefs. Here's another area where most of us have learned to settle for self-imposed limitations that will inevitably lead to self-imposed destinies. Often, such attitudes and limitations are expressed in statements like these:

> "I'm not good-looking. And nobody wants to spend time with someone who's not good-looking."

"I'm just a working-class stiff."

"I was never good in school. The smart people got ahead while I got stuck."

"I'm just not creative. I have no flair. I'm just a plodder."

"My life is not exciting, but it's good enough for a person like me."

"I'm not adventurous enough to start a business or be an entrepreneur. I'm destined to spend my life on the check-cashing line on payday at the bank."

"Only slim people who look good in suits get the really good jobs. I'm not one of them."

Pessimistic attitudes about other people. Negative attitudes about others don't hurt other people. They hurt us by limiting what we are willing to try. In extreme cases, our attitudes toward other people exert a paralyzing force on our lives. We think other people are blocking us or limiting our ability to move ahead.

Consider these statements:

"The human resources people at big corporations wouldn't even look at a résumé that came from someone my age. No point in applying."

"All the movers out there value good looks and money above everything else they look for in a lover or a spouse. They wouldn't take a second look at me."

Sometimes, limiting beliefs about other people take on a nearly paranoid aspect:

"Nobody ever gives me a chance."

"People are only looking out for themselves. They never help anyone unless they see something in it for them."

"The whole publishing world is so political. There's no point in sending out my new manuscript, since the only books that get published are written by people with political connections. It's a scratch-my-back-and-I'll-scratch-yours world out there."

The point is, such attitudes cause people to lose control of their lives. They are often referred to as "defeatist" attitudes. Whatever you choose to call them, they program you for failure.

Again, let's check in with Jacqueline, Doug, and Chris to see what they learned in completing Step 2.

- "I realized that I had a lot of limiting attitudes," says Jacqueline. "I saw that I blamed my weight on my parents, who were also heavy. I was unmotivated to lose weight because of my attitude, which said, 'Who would care if I did, anyway?' In this step, I realized that the point of losing weight would be that *I would care* after I'd done it. I saw that the reason to turn my situation around was to make myself happy, not other people."

- "In this step, I realized that I had conjured up a false feeling that people were 'ganging up' on shy people like me. Perhaps it dated from my days in high school and college, when I felt ostracized and disliked by people who were outgoing and popular. I also realized that these limiting beliefs really were holding me back from living the most enjoyable kind of life I could. Worst of all, they existed in my mind alone. Was anyone really out there saying, 'Let's ostracize Doug, he's so shy'? Of course not. The whole thing was an odd scenario I had generated to keep myself from making changes in my life."

- "I realized I had decided that nobody would give a job to someone my age," says Chris. "And once I realized how limiting that belief was, and how wrong, I began to consider the possibility that I could find a more interesting job if I really decided to."

STEP 3: SET GOALS FOR KEY CHANGE AREAS

It's time to set some goals in the key areas for change you've identified in Steps 1 and 2. In other words, it's time for some preliminary planning and testing in the areas you've identified where you would like your life to be a little—or a lot—better.

Remember, at this stage, you are still engaged in *preliminary* testing of broad outlines for meaningful life changes. It is not yet time to make specific, short-term plans to put your changes into motion. The overall goal at this point is to create simple goals that are realistic, heartfelt, and doable.

In this step, it is a very good idea to write things out. You'll find that, the moment you begin to put your plans and intentions on paper, they move out of the realm of the wistful and into the realm of planning. Here are some substeps to follow.

Write down your biggest hopes and goals. They might turn out to be something like these:

> "I want to find a job that brings me more excitement and satisfaction."
>
> "I don't want to be lonely so much of the time. I want to broaden my social circle."
>
> "I want to develop some deeper, more satisfying friendships instead of so many superficial ones."

"I want to experience more of the world through travel. And I want to do so while I am still robust enough to enjoy life."

"I want to get in better physical condition and feel better about myself."

"I want to find out whether I have what it takes to start a business of my own."

Talk your ideas over with people you are close to. Just let them in on what you are considering. "Bounce" your ideas off the people you trust the most and see what kind of information and opinions they give back to you.

In most cases, you will find that people encourage you. Even if they are not able or willing to put their personal seal of approval on the goal you have in mind, they will likely applaud you for trying to make positive changes in your life.

Let your goals mature and sink in. In this way—by letting your goals "sit" over a few months—you will be able to gain new perspective and dream up new ways to approach your goal. At the same time, you will ensure that the goals you are about to act on are authentic and valid for you—not frivolous or intended to fulfill the expectations of other people rather than your own.

How did Jacqueline, Doug, and Chris fare in Step 3? Let's hear from them.

- "I wrote down my goal: 'Finally and permanently lose at least 20 pounds,'" says Jacqueline, "and its specificity really scared me at first. But after I let it sit there and confront me for a few months, I realized it had validity for me—all the excuses aside. I talked it over with my sisters, one of whom told me, 'I know you'd be so much happier if you got that to happen. It's been a source of unhappiness for you for years.' So I felt much more ready to move ahead."

- "When I wrote down my goal to break my cycle of loneliness and isolation, it was kind of liberating in itself," says Doug. "To see it written there—well, it made me realize that the problem I was facing was pretty large and that it was no longer a good idea to ignore it. Then, when I mentioned my goal to my one close friend, he was very concerned for me. He said he was not even aware that I was lonely and he also pointed out that there was no reason for me to continue living in isolation and pain. Those events validated my goal and helped put it into focus as something valid that I really needed to try."

- Chris points to similar energizing benefits he realized from following this step: "I wrote down my goal—to find a new kind of work that would really excite and stimulate me. It suddenly felt like a large, new object in the middle of my life. Would I act on it? Hopefully. Even if not, there was no longer denying that I had to come to terms with my lack of satisfaction in my work, and not go on ignoring it."

STEP 4: GET GOING ON YOUR GOALS

Now it's time to set down some doable, short-term steps to let you begin to move toward your goals in the areas you've decided need change.

After all, unless you take this step—unless you begin to take action—your goals and desires can sit around and become negatives: "one more thing" you didn't do right. Yet if you can set out some actionable, short-term activities to help you move ahead, you can keep your wishes from turning into unfulfilled "monsters." And don't we all have some of those "monsters" sitting around our lives?

One fellow I know claimed for years that he wanted to become a millionaire. He set out that goal without breaking it down, and as a result, it became a brooding, self-restricting force in his life: something that never got done, that was only one more proof of his inadequacy. To break free of that, he would have needed to deal in specifics. Instead, he let his "big" dream remain unrealized.

Here are some steps to help you break down your dream and start moving toward it.

Make a list of things that need to be done. Try to become quite specific here. If you, like the man I describe above, would like to be a millionaire, your steps might include:

> "I will make a budget and see if there is somewhere I can spend a few hundred dollars less each month. I could then invest that money."

> "I will investigate courses about investing and take one so I can learn the basics."

> "I will visit a bookstore and buy some basic books on building wealth."

> "I will speak with a financial planner and get some advice on retirement planning."

Create some steps, dates, and deadlines. You need to do this to keep your goals from retreating ever into the future. The best approach? Attack your change areas in small, doable steps that you can comfortably accomplish in and around your other life activities. Even in a busy week, after all, you can make a quick call to ask about a class or club. Or you can stop by a library, or visit the Internet, to do some research.

Remember, you can't expect to transform your life completely in a month or two. But what you *can* do—and this is certainly more important—is *start moving ahead* in areas where you really desire to change.

Jacqueline, Doug, and Chris all report similar progress in this step.

- "I determined I would buy one new cookbook with low-fat, low-calorie recipes each month and try out its recipes through the month," Jacqueline says. "Preferably, it would present some spicy ethnic cuisine to keep me interested and not feeling deprived."

- "I decided I would broaden my social circle a little at a time," Doug explains. "Each month, I would call up two people and ask them to join me for lunch. I would start with older friends and, once I became comfortable with that, I would enlarge the circle enough to include other people I didn't know as well. In a year or two, I envisioned, I might even have a dinner party in my home with five or six friends. But for the moment, I'd start small."

- "I called up a vocational counselor—a very big step for me—and made an appointment," says Chris. This represents a breakthrough for Chris. Only a few months ago, after all, he was saying that people were supposed to be content with dull jobs! Now he's taking positive steps to break out of such a job and find more enjoyment in his work.

STEP 5: EXAMINE YOUR RESISTANCE

As you reached Step 4, you probably encountered a somewhat unpleasant surprise. Something was holding you back
from bringing about change in your life in the areas where
you needed it most! You discovered you were comfortable
staying stuck in negative routines—sometimes so comfortable that making changes seemed nearly impossible.

Or you might have found that you were resisting change
in old, familiar ways. As Jacqueline summarizes it, "I had
already tried to lose weight so many times that I actually
knew the resistance points that I would encounter. I'd 'fall
off the wagon' more than once by overeating. Then I'd blame
myself. Then I'd teeter on the edge of giving up entirely. In
the past, I'd always lose out to these points of resistance and,
in the end, I'd be right back where I had started without having made any changes at all."

Making meaningful change in our lives is never easy.
Since we encounter resistance at every step along the way,
this is a critical stage. Unless we navigate our way through
resistance successfully, we will be unable to make any meaningful change in the areas we have defined.

Still, there are some steps we can take to move through
this phase successfully—perilous though it might seem.

Examine the blame. When we fail to make progress in
important life-changing areas, blame is usually part of the
picture. We blame other people or outer circumstances by
telling ourselves things like these:

> "I have to cook for my husband, and he's not on a
> diet. No way he'll diet along with me as I try to lose
> weight. I have no support for what I'm trying to do."

> "I have no privacy at work. How am I supposed to make some phone calls to examine other career options. I'm just too boxed in."

> "I have so many bills coming due over the next few months that there is no way I can make a financial plan. Maybe in a few months I can, when things clear up."

Write down such excuses, take a look at them, and decide whether they represent valid reasons to remain immobilized. Once you confront your excuses, it becomes harder to hide from them.

Is the fact that your spouse is not on a diet an excuse to remain overweight yourself, for example? Or is the fact that some bills are due really a justification for not doing some financial planning? Not really. Excuses, more often than not, are simply justifications for remaining stuck in comfortable ruts.

Determine what, if anything, has stopped you in the past. Again, write everything down. This is particularly important if you are trying to make a life change for the second or third time. If you're trying to set up a program of saving—something you tried in the past several times, and failed—write down an explanation of why. Then examine what you have written and decide whether it is really reason enough to stay stuck in your life.

Examine the discomfort and accept it. Every life change causes discomfort:

> "Going to the gym and putting on exercise clothes is embarrassing. Worse yet, my muscles ache like crazy the day afterward."

"My friends at work are poking fun at me for trying to diet. They make it hard for me to continue."

"I'm not used to budgeting. Last weekend when my wife and I were invited out to dinner with some friends, I had to tell them we were trying to economize and save money. It was embarrassing."

The interesting thing is, when we analyze and accept such discomfort for what it is—when we are able to say openly, "This will hurt for a little while, like a new pair of shoes"—we free ourselves to act despite the discomfort and awkwardness. We become able to make statements like these:

"I'll have aching muscles for a week or two, and then that will be a thing of the past."

"I'll just have to put up with jibes from friends at work about my dieting, and then they will lose interest."

"Good friends can understand when times are tight. We can still have dinners together at the local family restaurant, maybe with an occasional splurge."

This stage, in fact, may be the most critical of all in making the life changes you desire. Let's see how Jacqueline, Doug, and Chris fared.

- "I was forced to confront the excuses and negative patterns I'd established in previous attempts to lose weight," Jacqueline admits. "Somehow, each time, I'd just get sloppy about my diet and fall back into self-destructive patterns of eating. I'd just lose steam. Yet this time, by analyzing and understanding my past, I stood a better chance of making successful change occur."

- "I saw that blame had become something of a filter through which I viewed other people and the world as a whole," Doug admits. "Rather than pointing a finger at myself for my failure to live a richer social life, I was throwing the blame entirely onto other people. *They* didn't like me. *They* didn't think I was interesting. *They* didn't take the initiative to invite me to social gatherings. *They* weren't warm and caring. All this blame represented something I was using to justify my own failure to make my life better."

- "I saw that my own intense pride was really holding me back," Chris states. "I was more influenced by my need to keep up appearances—that everything was normal, that everything was under control—than by my need to make some needed career changes. Fear of appearing uncertain or insecure had immobilized me into complete inaction in the areas of my life where change was needed the most."

STEP 6: TAKE COURAGE

In this step, you identify and tap into the sources of support and courage you'll need to successfully complete your journey. Here are several suggestions.

Look for mentors who can support you. Seek out people who have successfully undertaken change processes that are similar to your own:

- If you're starting to exercise, connect with someone who has managed to do so. In many cases, it's most effective to find someone who has overcome obstacles similar to your own.

One newcomer to exercise found the perfect mentor at a local YMCA—a woman who was remarkably fit and motivated to exercise, and who, like herself, was a working mother. "By talking with her," the newcomer explained, "I gained insights I could use. Certainly more useful insights than I would have if I had chosen a professional athlete as a role model."

- If you're trying to move from teaching into a job in business—or vice versa—try to network your way to someone who has made a similar transaction in his or her life.

- If you're trying to start a business of your own, talk to someone much like yourself who has done so. Explain what your ambitions are and listen to whatever advice your mentor has to offer.

Take yourself right to the edge of your fears and confront them. Often, the most effective way to break fear's hold is to confront it directly. Consider these statements from people who have done just that:

- "I was afraid of flying in airplanes, and that fear was imposing some very crippling limits on both my career and my enjoyment of life. I went to see a psychotherapist, who recommended that I try a behavior modification program. I was terrified, but I found such a program and signed up. That was the first step toward conquering my fears."

- "After my husband and I were mugged, we lived in fear every time we went out for dinner or a movie. We resolved that we had to do something, so we signed up for a martial-arts class. How uncomfortable it was to go to that first class! But as soon as we started to learn some self-defense techniques, it felt liberating."

- "I was afraid to express interest in men—*really* afraid. But one day, I decided to telephone a man I had met at a party the week before and see if he wanted to go to a concert with me. It was terrifying. But I did call him and we've gone out a few times. I feel that a great weight has been lifted off my shoulders. Fear of the unknown is much worse than the discomfort of dealing with reality. After all, asking someone for a date isn't asking him to marry you. You're only asking to spend a few pleasant hours together and have a good time."

Keep practicing and stretching your courage. Think of courage as a muscle. If you keep working it, it will grow stronger over time. As with the woman quoted above, who became quite comfortable in expressing interest in members of the opposite sex, keep practicing. Things that seemed difficult or impossible only a short time ago may be strengthened to the point that they become a normal way of "doing business" with the world.

How did Jacqueline, Doug, and Chris fare at this stage? Very well, as revealed in these statements from them.

- "I got comfortable with the notion of cooking lean, healthy foods and eating them alongside any other entrees my family members were enjoying," says Jacqueline. "Sometimes, my kids like what I am eating more than what is on their plates. The result has been that we are often enjoying lighter meals as a family— a grilled piece of fish, a salad with some lean meat and tofu, or a casserole with grains and beans. I didn't believe we could ever accomplish such a profound change in our habits, but we did."

- "I've gotten more comfortable asking people to join me in social activities," says Doug. "It felt awkward at first, but it's nearly second nature to me now."

- "Sure, it was awkward admitting that I wanted to change careers," says Chris, "and it was embarrassing telling my family that I would be moving into a new job and possibly earning a bit less money for a while. Yet I had to take those steps in order to free myself to change."

STEP 7: ENJOY THE FRUITS OF YOUR EFFORT

If you've made a major change through this Seven-Step Action Plan to Take Control of Your Life, take a little time to congratulate yourself on a job well done.

Gather some friends together and let them help you celebrate. It's something that Jacqueline did after she had lost 15 pounds. "My family and friends were eager to express their support," she says.

Find ways to deepen your commitment to your goal. I know a casual jogger who has evolved into a marathoner. I also know a woman who overcame high blood pressure through weight loss, exercise, and healthy foods; she has become something of an expert on vitamins and mineral supplements.

When you've accomplished the change you envisioned, seeking new levels to explore not only sustains your interest but also makes your change an integral part of your way of interacting with the world.

Find organizations or support groups. There are groups that will support you in the changes you have made—ranging from cooking clubs to bicycling organizations to groups that support people who have overcome a wide range of addictions or negative behaviors. Becoming involved is energizing and positive. Plus, the support such groups provide minimizes the chances of falling back into negative patterns.

Start new change processes too. If you've lost weight, you can begin to exercise to improve your level of aerobic conditioning. If you've made a successful career change, it might be a good time to take a fresh look at your retirement planning and get *that* house in order. If you've overcome social awkwardness, it might be time to learn more about fashion and improve your sense of style.

New vistas are always there! And by applying the Seven-Step Action Plan when and where you decide, you will find you can come a lot closer to reaching the elusive goal of taking control of your life.

FURTHER READING

The Accidental Buddhist: Mindfulness, Enlightenment, and Sitting Still by Dinty W. Moore. Algonquin Books, 1997.

Altering Fate: Why the Past Does Not Predict the Future by Michael Lewis. Guilford Press, 1997.

Am I a Hindu? The Hinduism Primer by Ed Viswanathan. Halo Books, 1992.

The Art of Modeling Dynamic Systems: Forecasting for Chaos, Randomness, and Determinism by Foster Morrison. John Wiley & Sons, 1991.

Bad Bet: The Inside Story of the Glamour, Glitz, and Danger of America's Gambling Industry by Timothy L. O'Brien. Times Books, 1998.

The Best of Luck to You by Murray Meszaros. A.M. Media, 1996.

The Bhagavad Gita edited by Juan Mascaro and Thomas Wyatt. Penguin Classics, 1983.

A Brief Introduction to Hinduism: Religion, Philosophy, and Ways of Liberation by A.L. Herman, Westview Press, 1991.

Chance and Chaos by David Ruelle. Princeton University Press, 1993.

Chance Rules: An Informal Guide to Probability, Risk, and Statistics by Brian Everitt. Springer Verlag, 1999.

Chaos: The Making of a New Science by James Gleick. Penguin Books, 1988.

Classics in Game Theory edited by Harold W. Kuhn. Princeton University Press, 1997.

The Collapse of Chaos: Discovering Simplicity in a Complex World by Jack Cohen and Ian Stewart. Penguin Books, 1995.

Complexity: The Emerging Science at the Edge of Order and Chaos by M. Mitchell Waldrop. Touchstone Books, 1993.

Crapped Out: How Gambling Is Ruining the Economy and Destroying Lives edited by Jennifer Vogel. Common Courage Press, 1997.

Creating Modern Probability: Its Mathematics, Physics, and Philosophy in Historical Perspective by Jan Von Plato. Cambridge University Press, 1998.

Creativity: Flow and the Psychology of Discovery and Invention by Mihaly Csikszentmihalyi. HarperCollins Books, 1997.

Dimensions of Karma edited by S.S. Rama Rao Pappu. South Asia Books, 1987.

Does God Play Dice? The Mathematics of Chaos by Ian Stewart. Blackwell Publishing, 1990.

Emergence of Probability: A Philosophical Study of Early Ideas About Probability by Ian Hacking. Cambridge University Press, 1984.

Exploring Chaos: A Guide to the New Science of Disorder edited by Nina Hall. W.W. Norton & Company, 1994.

Finding Flow: The Psychology of Engagement with Everyday Life by Mihaly Csikszentmihalyi. Basic Books, 1998.

Flow: The Psychology of Optimal Experience by Mihaly Csikszentmihalyi. HarperCollins Books, 1991.

Frontiers of Complexity: The Search for Order in a Chaotic World by Peter Coveney and Roger Highfield. Fawcett Books, 1996.

Frontiers of Game Theory by Ken Binmore, Alan Kirman, and Piero Tani. MIT Press, 1993.

Game Theory: A Nontechnical Introduction by Morton D. Davis. Dover Publications, 1997.

Games, Gods, and Gambling: A History of Probability and Statistical Ideas by F. N. David. Dover Publications, 1998.

How to Make Luck: The Seven Secrets Lucky People Use to Succeed by Marc Myers. Renaissance Books, 1999.

Impossibility: The Limits of Science and the Science of Limits by John D. Barrow. Oxford University Press, 1998.

Karma Manual: Nine Ways to Change Your Life by John Mumford, Meghan Stevens, and Anandakapila Saraswati. Llewellyn Publications, 1999.

FURTHER READING

Laws of the Game: How the Principles of Nature Govern Chance by Manfred Eigen and Ruthild Winkler. Princeton University Press, 1993.

Leadership and the New Science by Margaret J. Wheatley. Berrett-Koehler Books, 1992.

The Luck Business: The Devastating Consequences and Broken Promises of America's Gambling Explosion by Robert Goodman. Free Press, 1996.

Luck: The Brilliant Randomness of Everyday Life by Nicholas Resher. Farrar Straus & Giroux, 1995.

The Power of Flow: Practical Ways to Transform Your Life with Meaningful Coincidence by Meg Lundstrom and Charlene Belitz. Three Rivers Press, 1998.

Randomness by Deborah J. Bennett. Harvard University Press, 1998.

The Taming of Chance by Tim Hacking and Ian Hacking. Cambridge University Press, 1990.

There Are No Accidents: Synchronicity and the Stories of Our Lives by Robert Hopcke. Riverhead Books, 1997.

INDEX

INDEX

INDEX

About the Authors

Dr. Richard Shoup is a psychotherapist, Presbyterian minister, and cofounder of the Vocare Group, which offers seminars on career transformation using spiritual and psychological tools. He is a recognized authority on bringing a new perspective to career transitions, human relationships, and life change.

Barry Lenson has written over 10 books, including *Simple Steps* (with Dr. Arthur Caliandro) and *Selling to the New America* (with Alfred L. Schreiber).

Introducing... The Vocare Group

If you liked some of the ideas in this book...continue your journey
with the products and services of The Vocare Group

Dr. Richard Shoup, author of *Take Control of Your Life*, is a principal of The Vocare Group, a unique team of three colleagues and counselors who share a belief in the importance of integrating spirituality with the challenges posed by the career and personal transitions we all face throughout our lives.

The Emergent Self: Consultation Services

The Vocare Group can work with you personally on many vital areas pertaining to work: career transition, skills identification, vocational discernment, interview coaching, and much more. We have various packages that include consultation, coaching, and follow-up. Call 212-585-2722 for more information or check the box on the order form.

Where Do I Go from Here?: An Inspirational Guide to Making Authentic Career and Life Choices
by Dr. Kenneth Ruge. Book: $12.95

A personal roadmap to connecting with your true self and tapping the power within you.

Finding Your Path: The Vocare Workshop
2 tapes plus workbook: $29.95

If you can't get to a Vocare workshop in person, ordering this set of tapes is the best way to go deeper in your search for your personal mission. You will be guided through a unique process designed to uncover your true desires and gifts, understand past influences, and help you respond to the call of new directions. Accompanied by an interactive workbook journal.

Opportunity Thinking
by Dr. Richard Shoup. 2 tapes: $15.95

Taking the phenomena of chaos, luck, karma, and grace, Dr. Shoup looks at ways each of us can make the most out of what life gives us.

Responsibility Thinking
by Dr. Richard Shoup. 2 tapes: $15.95

Reframing our lives in terms of personal leadership, Dr. Shoup looks at responsibility as a way to make an effective response to the challenges life brings.

Deepening Your Spirituality
by Dr. Kenneth Ruge. 2 tapes: $15.95

An inspiring and practical discussion of ways you can go deeper in your spiritual journey, with useful suggestions on daily practices.

Prayer: Beyond the First Steps
by Nina H. Frost. 2 tapes: $15.95

How can prayer be an integral part of our lives? How do we pray in times of transition or loss? This series makes many aspects of prayer accessible in simple, powerful ways you can use.

Where Am I Going, God?
by Nina H. Frost. 2 tapes: $15.95

How can you feel God's guidance in your everyday life? In your choice of work, in relationships, in decision making? This wide-ranging series uncovers many clues that help you discern what you are called to do in your spiritual journey.

Wrestling with Your Angel
by Dr. Kenneth Ruge. 2 tapes: $15.95

How can you find the courage and endurance to grapple with your particular life challenge? Here are a variety of spiritual and psychological tools to help you take heart and wrestle with your angel.

Money, Sex, and Power
by Dr. Kenneth Ruge. 2 tapes: $15.95

Money, sex, and power are cultural icons which can seduce us from a true and authentic path. Dr. Ruge offers insight and spiritual leverage to help you put your life in the proper perspective.

Listen to Your Dreams
by Dr. Kenneth Ruge. 2 tapes: $15.95

Dreams offer us a gateway to the wisdom of the unconscious mind. Unlock the meanings of your dreams and tap the power of the unconscious.

Additional copies of *Take Control of Your Life*
are available by calling the publisher at 1-800-722-4726.

CALL 1 800-345-6665
ORDER FORM

Qty.	Title	Cost	Amount
	Where Do I Go from Here?	$12.95	
	Finding Your Path: The Vocare Workshop	$29.95	
	Opportunity Thinking	$15.95	
	Responsibility Thinking	$15.95	
	Deepening Your Spirituality	$15.95	
	Prayer: Beyond the First Steps	$15.95	
	Where Am I Going, God?	$15.95	
	Wrestling with Your Angel	$15.95	
	Money, Sex, and Power	$15.95	
	Listen to Your Dreams	$15.95	
	Special offer! **Finding Your Path: The Vocare Workshop** *plus any 2 companion tape titles listed (regularly $61.85)*	$49.95	

	Subtotal	
Shipping/ $0-$16.........$4.00 *Foreign*		
Handling $17-$45........$6.50 *shipments,* *Shipping & Handling*		
$46 + ...$8.50 *please call.* *Total Enclosed*		

Please charge my
VISA/MasterCard #:   *Expires:*

Ship to: (please print)

Name

Address

City   *State*   *Zip*

Phone (   )   *Fax (   )*

Make checks payable to Pathway Book Service
Mail orders: Send to Pathway Book Service, 4 White Brook Rd., Gilsum, NH 03448
Fax orders: Fax to 603-357-2073   *Telephone orders:* Call 1-800-345-6665
E-mail orders: pbs@top.monad.net

FREE INFORMATION

For ❏ free information on *The Emergent Self:* **Consultation Services**
or ❏ to be on our mailing list, just call 212-585-2722.
You can also fax us at 212-717-8227, or e-mail us at vocaregrp@aol.com or
mail your address to The Vocare Group, P.O. Box 2448, New York, NY 10021.